Fly-Fishing Guide To The Great Smoky Mountains

Fly-Fishing Guide To The Great Smoky Mountains

Don Kirk

Menasha Ridge Press
Birmingham, Alabama

Published by Menasha Ridge Press
Distributed by The Globe Pequot Press
First edition, third printing, 2002

Cover photo by Joanna Kirk
Cover design by Grant Tatum
Book design by Brian Caskey

Library of Congress Cataloging-in-Publication Data
Kirk, Don, 1952—
    [Fly-fishing guide to the Great Smoky Mountains]
    Kirk's fly-fishing guide to the Great Smoky Mountains/Don Kirk.
—1st ed.
        p.   cm.
    Includes Index.
    ISBN 0-89732-235-5
    1. Fly fishing—Great Smoky Mountains National Park (N.C.
and Tenn.) I. Title.
SH456.K44   1996
799.1'757'0976889—dc21

                                                        96-48482
                                                        CIP

Menasha Ridge Press
P.O. Box 43673
Birmingham, Alabama 35243
www.menasharidge.com

Contents

Acknowledgments

This revised version of the original book is the result of several years of effort. Many hours were spent pouring over old Park records and maps, and conducting interviews to ensure depth and accuracy of the information. Without the aid and support of a number of people, this project could not have been completed.

All National Park Service personnel contacted were very helpful. In particular, Stewart (Stu) Coleman gave generously of his time and provided essential information. Alan Kelley of the U.S. Fish and Wildlife Service furnished material on brook trout and the Cades Cove area. Robert Smith, also of the U.S. Fish and Wildlife Service, supplied technical data and research tips. Uplands Laboratory's Ray Matthews provided information concerning Abrams Creek, and Steve Moore of Uplands Laboratory was kind enough to review the book's outline.

Technical information on feeding habits of the trout of the area was provided by Price Wilkinson, former fishery biologist for the Tennessee Wildlife Resource Agency. Price also checked the outline of the book. Good friend and fishing buddy Marc Sudheimer contributed encouragement.

Dr. David Etnier of the Department of Zoology at the University of Tennessee looked over my outline, and furnished valuable information on caddisflies.

Ben Craig and Eddie George, the region's two top fly crafters, generously shared their vast knowledge of fly-fishing with me. Greg Ward, owner of Rocky Outfitters in Pigeon Forge, Tennessee gets a truly special thanks for not only providing fresh insight into some areas of fly-fishing in the park, but also for pointing out the need for this version of the book for to a number of reasons, not the least of which was the impending production of two other fly-fishing guides to the streams of the Great Smoky Mountains National Park.

Much of the historical background could never have been assembled without the cooperation of a number of fine folks from the western Carolinas and eastern Tennessee. Space does not permit the mention of all who contributed, but among those who must be mentioned is Walter Cole of Gatlinburg. Walter spent a warm morning in May with me on his front porch, telling me of the mountains and the men of his youth. Ernest Ramsey of Pigeon Forge provided me with a wealth of information concerning his years spent guiding fishermen in the Smokies, building split cane rods and tying flies. Jack Shuttle, owner of a tackle shop in Newport, tied and explained a score of Smoky Mountain flies for me. Wendell Crisp, a Bryson City tackle shop owner, also provided information on North Carolina fly patterns, and shared his memories of when he was a boy living in Proctor. Kirk Jenkins of Newport provided me with a number of superbly tied Yallarhammars and Little River Ants, as well as vital stream information. Jim Ellison of Morristown shared the tactics and flies he developed for fishing such difficult waters as the Greenbriar. Jim Mills, a top-notch fly tyer and fly-fisherman, also assisted in my research.

Mr. Olin Watson, former president of the Smoky Mountains Historical Society, was kind enough to share some tales recalled from the days he hunted and fished the ridges of the Smokies.

Information concerning the Cherokee Indians was furnished by Duane King, director of the Museum of the Cherokee Indians, and Adam Thompson, stocking coordinator for the Cherokee Fish and Game Management Enterprise.

Sam Venable and my son Jeff Kirk accompanied me on several photographic trips in the Park. George Keener assisted with advice on photographic problems. Susan Fliegel, my assistant editor at Thicket Publishing, helped make sure everything was grammatical and correctly spelled.

My sincere thanks to all who gave of their time, expertise, and knowledge to the compilation of this book.

Introduction

The Great Smoky Mountains National Park offers one of the last wild trout habitats in the eastern United States. Annually, millions of Americans visit this natural wonderland seeking recreation and a chance to enjoy the outdoors. Among these visitors are thousands of anglers eager to test their luck against the stream bred trout of the park's famed waters. Most of these anglers lack the needed information, and are confused by the seemingly endless number of streams available.

Somewhere in the early seventies when my children where young (as was I), the idea of writing a trout fishing guide to the streams of the Great Smoky Mountains National Park first crossed my mind. It took a few more years of fishing, then several years of work before that book was published in 1981. Since that time, *Trout Fishing Guide To The Smokies* has been a raving success that has been revised and reprinted many times. Few endeavors have netted me so many compliments as that little guidebook.

Many things have changed over the last two decades in the Great Smoky Mountains National Park. Regulations have changed radically, and fishing pressure on many streams has increased dramatically. Guide services available to anglers wishing to sample park waters were virtually non-existent when my book was first written, as were fly-fishing shops within 50 miles of the park. That also has changed. Both the shops and guide services are now relatively common in the Smokies. The city of Gatlinburg even promotes fishing for trout, something that was unheard of only a few years ago.

This book is designed to help both experienced and novice anglers select waters that suit their tastes and abilities. You will find a chapter on each of the major streams in the park. Listed with each stream are such valuable data as its location, fishing pressure, species of trout found in that particular watershed, both auto and trail access routes, campsite accommodations, and other information. Also included are chapters covering the early history of trout fishing in the park, information on the aquatic insects most abundant in the streams, proven dry and wet nymph patterns, tips on gear, fly-fishing, and so on. In the Great Smoky Mountains National Park, we have some of the finest trout fishing anywhere. And although the trout are wary, even a beginner can expect to catch a few.

The Great Smoky Mountains National Park has long been one of the country's most popular fly-fishing destinations. This book represents at least the fourth attempt by an ardent angler to provide fellow fishermen with information on catching trout from these streams. The first book written on fishing in the Smokies was penned in 1937 by then park ranger, Joe F. Manley. Manley, who was employed by the National Park Service for only two years before accepting employment in Gatlinburg as chief of their water works department, was an avid fisherman. His eighty-page, hard-bound title was vanity published one time to the tune of three thousand volumes according to Manley, who I spoke to last in 1990 at his home in Gatlinburg. This rare and little-known book is unknown to most anglers, but was brought to my attention in 1987 by noted Smoky Mountain angler Eddie George of Louisville, Tennessee, who could rightly be termed the best fly-fisherman to ever cast these streams.

According to Manley, shortly after his book, *Fishing Guide to the Smokies*, was printed, he agreed to guide an editor from either *Field and Stream* or *Outdoor Life* magazine (he could not recall precisely which). During the course of their fishing trips, Manley shared information on his book with the northerner, who bought and took home his entire printing. Only a few dozen of these books were ever sold locally.

Manley's book contains interesting information on the streams of the Smokies, and is about equally split between trout and bass fishing. One of the most interesting photographs of the book depicts Manley at the Sinks on Little River holding up a stringer of smallmouth bass weighing between 3 and 5 pounds. His favorite flyrod "lure," a Heddon-made Flaptail, can still be found at antique tackle shows at a cost of forty to eighty dollars. Can you imagine how quickly most of us would climb a tree to retrieve one of these costly little jewels? If you can find a copy of Manley's book for less than two hundred dollars, do not hesitate to part with the cash. It is harder to find than eyebrows on a brook trout.

The second book written on this subject was the effort of Jim Gasque, a somewhat prolific writer from western North Carolina. This title, *Hunting and Fishing in the Great Smokies*, was published by Alfred A. Knopf of New York, who at the same time published other well-known sporting titles such as *Trout* by Ray Bergman, *Ruffed Grouse* by John Alden Knight, and *A Book of Duck Shooting* by Van Campen Heilner. *Hunting and Fishing in the Great Smokies* and Gasque's other, better-known title, *Bass Fishing*, can still be found on book lists circulated among collectors of vintage fishing tackle and associated paraphernalia. Published in 1948, Gasque's book was the first nationally-distributed book on fishing in (and around) the Smokies, although Horace Kephart, who also was a great fan of angling these waters, often wrote about it as well.

Gasque's book immortalized the great western North Carolina angler, Mark Cathey, who this author was born too late to make the acquaintance of. *Hunting and Fishing in the Great Smokies* is a gem worth the current asking price of fifty to one hundred dollars. Written in the folksy, "me 'n Joe" style of outdoor writing common to the era, it provides more in the way entertainment than information, although the techniques and few flies noted in the book are as deadly on trout today as when the information was penned half a century ago. Gasque's chapters on Cataloochee and Deep creeks are extremely insightful.

The third book written on trout fishing in the Great Smoky Mountains National Park is perhaps the rarest of all of the four titles known to me. Discovered when going through the National Park Service archives in 1979, *Sport Fishing The Smokies* by Joe Manley is an extremely short, but very accurate book on the ins and outs of catching trout in the Smokies. Only sixteen pages long, this informative book was published in 1969, and apparently had only a very short shelf life. My favorite notation in the book was when the author advised anglers looking for bigger trout to use techniques that took their flies deep along the bottom. How right Manley was.

The fourth book written on fishing for trout in the Great Smoky Mountains National Park was an effort I began in the mid-1970s as a young man with an unquenchable thirst for catching fish from these pristine waters. The first printing of one thousand books was published by McGuire/Denton Publishers of Dayton, Ohio. It was the first comprehensive, stream-by-stream guide to the thirteen major watersheds in the park. This white, blue, and black paperback has become something of a collectible in its own right. I own only three copies and can only guess what the publishers did with the remaining inventory.

In 1984 Menasha Ridge Press of Birmingham, Alabama, acquired rights to that book, *Trout Fishing Guide to the Smokies*. It was revised, with chapters added to include the waters in the Cherokee Indian Reservation located east of the national park, as well as the five lakes that border the southern portion of the Smokies. Now known as *Smoky Mountains Trout Fishing Guide*, this book has been extremely well-received. It is currently in its tenth printing.

Naturally, other books have been written that include considerable information on fly-fishing in the Great Smoky Mountains. My close friend and mentor, Charley "Chum" Dickey (who is from my hometown), wrote a book with Freddie Moses (a noted fly-fishing attorney from Knoxville, Tennessee) titled *Trout Fishing*. Published by Oxmoor House, this tough-to-find title from the 1960s is one of my most cherished possessions.

Other books you might wish to locate on this subject include *Papa Was A Fisherman: Memories of the Great Smokies* by Joe B. Long (1969), *Twenty Years Hunting and Fishing in the Great Smokies* by Sam Hunnicutt, and *On The Spine of Time; An Angler's Love of the Smokies* by another personal friend, Harry Middleton (1991).

The only complaint I have received about my previous books on fishing in the Smokies (with the exception that they revealed too many formerly-secret fishing spots to interloping Yankees) was the inclusion of the spinner fishing information. My goal when writing *Smoky Mountains Trout Fishing Guide* was to enable as many would-be anglers as possible to find waters that best suited their needs and to tell those unfamiliar with catching trout from these streams how it might be accomplished. The downside of my efforts was, to put it as frankly as possible, that I ruffled the feathers of the growing number of fly-fishing purists. Over the last fifteen years I have spoken at many Trout Unlimited and Federation of Fly Fishermen events, only to hear catty remarks for having included the habits of the scum of the earth, that is, those who enjoy spinner fishing, in such a book. Thus, we come full circle to one of the key reasons this title is now offered.

In the future there may be other fly-fishing guides to the Smokies, but this is the first and undeniably the most comprehensive. Even if it does not make any money, it has already provided me with over fourteen dozen excuses to plan trout fishing trips to the streams of the Great Smoky Mountains National Park.

Naturally, this book was written by me in part as an effort to convert my knowledge of these wonderful waters and fly-fishing the Smokies into monetary gain. If you have read this far, it is safe to assume you have already plunked your money down. However, that is not the only reason. For years I wanted anglers from all over to come sample the incredible fishing found here. More than anything, this book and other fishing books I have written are an effort on my part to entice others to come share the joy of the great outdoors.

Tight lines,

Don Kirk
Morristown, Tennessee
1996

Chapter 1

Smoky Mountains Trout and Bass

The majestic Great Smoky Mountains National Park is a rugged half-million-acre wilderness sanctuary located on the border between Tennessee and North Carolina. Encompassed in the park are several steep, tree-lined ridges, separated by deep valleys. There are more than 700 miles of cool, crystal-clear streams.

One of the most diverse biospheres on earth, the Smokies range from an elevation of 850 feet at the mouth of Abrams Creek to 6,642 feet on Clingman's Dome. The flora are incredibly diverse, with several trees reaching their record growth in the park. There are thirteen major watersheds in the Smokies, as well as a number of smaller ones. These streams range in size from the largest, the Little River and Oconaluftee River, which during periods of normal flow are big enough to float a canoe down, to an almost endless number of small headwater rills. Living in these streams is a wide spectrum of aquatic insects and invertebrates, as well as more than seventy species of fish, including darters, suckers, dace, shiners, chubs, scuplins, bream, bass, and the native brook trout. Since the turn of the century, two other species, the rainbow trout and the brown trout, have become part of the ecosystem of the Smokies, although they are considered "exotics" by fisheries biologists.

The Brook Trout (Salvelinus fontinalis)

The brook trout, known affectionately to the mountain folk of the Smokies as the "spec," is not a true trout, but a char. The world's trout—salmon, grayling, and whitefish—are members of one homogeneous group. The trout, in turn, are divided into two technically separate groups, the true trout and the chars.

This classification is arrived at principally through skeletal structure, teeth, and scale differences. This is of little importance to anglers, as the more apparent differences in coloration are

Brook char, or speckle trout, are the only native cold-water game fish of the Smokies.

obvious. Chars always have a dark background color with light spots. True trout, such as the rainbow and brown, always have a light background color with dark spots.

The brook trout is distinctive from other fish with its "worm like" markings on its back (known as vermiculations) and white-edged lower fins. The brook trout, like all chars, spawns in the fall.

In the Smokies, the brook trout feed on numerous forms of aquatic insects, including stoneflies, mayflies, and caddis flies. Terrestrial insects are also an important part of their diet, and include bees, wasps, beetles, ants, jassids, flies, and grasshoppers. Crayfish are important daily fare, as are minnows. The brook trout is capable of digesting a stomachful of food in less than half an hour, a fact that prods the brookie to constantly look out for almost any edible morsels.

The brookies of the Smokies were "marooned" here after the glacial epoch. Originally an ocean-dwelling fish from the Arctic, the brook trout migrated down the eastern seacoast, fleeing the freezing onslaught of the ensuing Ice Age. When the rivers had cooled sufficiently to offer suitable habitat, the brookies moved upstream and established themselves. As the rivers began to warm, the brook trout were forced to retreat into the cool mountain headwaters.

The brook trout was once abundant in the Smokies. Accounts of fishing trips made into the mountains prior to 1890 tell of fish being caught by the hundreds. Large-scale logging operations came into the Smokies in the late 1890s. Whole watersheds were logged out, dams were erected on the streams, railroad lines were built up alongside many streams, and fires fed on the slash left behind by the timber-cutting operations: these were but some of the devastating problems the brook trout faced. All logging operations ceased in 1935 (approximately two-thirds of the Smokies were logged during this period), and better land management helped heal the wounds left by the previous forty years.

Rainbow trout were introduced into every major stream in the Smokies during this period. Massive stockings of rainbow trout were continued through 1947. The brook trout, which lost over half of its original range to the loggers, is now losing additional territory to the rainbow trout. Why the brook trout cannot regain its lost range where habitat conditions have returned to near-normal, and what part the rainbow trout plays in this drama, are not fully understood. Several explanations have been offered, and research into the dilemma continues. A moratorium was placed on the killing of brook trout in the park in 1975. Scores of headwater streams were closed (and remain so at this writing) to protect the remaining brookies.

Considerable debate remains not over the future of the brook trout in the streams of the Great Smoky Mountains National Park, but also whether these fish are indeed a unique subspecies of brook trout. A couple of streams in the park (at the headwaters of Little River) where brookies are found re-opened a few years ago. This was due to management efforts to prevent rainbow encroachment. Prevention of the ascent of rainbows into brook trout waters appears to help the brookie. In the nearby Cherokee National Forest the combined efforts of the U.S. Forest Service and Trout Unlimited have almost doubled the amount of brook trout water by actively working to improve brook trout habitat.

A recent study published by the University of Tennessee ended the long standing debate regarding whether the brook trout of Southern Appalachia are indeed genetically unique. Pure southern-strain brook trout do exist, and in some locales are doing remarkably well. Where northern brook trout have been introduced, and in the Great Smoky Mountain National Park this covers nearly all watersheds, northern-strain brookies and southern-strain/northern-strain hybrids are common. It is not uncommon for northern- and southern-strain brookies to occupy the same waters.

There is considerable debate regarding the future of the southern brook trout. Their average life expectancy is three years or less, which does not work to their advantage. Whether or not they are being assaulted more these days by factors such as acid rain and global warming, two suggestions I personally do not buy into, is a matter of enlightened conjecture. Pressure from rainbow and brown trout is the primary problem.

In order to save the brook trout of the Great Smoky Mountains National Park, the National Park Service may ultimately need to take more aggressive management approaches. This does not necessarily mean closing waters to fishing.

The Rainbow Trout (Salmo gairdneri)

The very name of this fish rings out with a surge of raw energy and beauty. The rainbow is well known for unsurpassed fighting ability, arching leaps, and superb eating quality. A powerful downstream run by one of these fish that rips the line from your reel will make you feel as if your heart is trying to bypass your Adam's apple.

The rainbow trout's original range extended from California to Bristol Bay in Alaska. This fish prefers fast, oxygenated water. Recognizable by its silvery flanks slashed with scarlet and its greenish back, the rainbow is a beautiful fish. Predominantly an insect eater, particularly in the streams of the Smokies, the rainbow will, however, strike spinners and minnow imitations with gusto.

Rainbow trout from the Sierra Mountains of California were shipped to Michigan in 1878. In a few years the adaptable western natives were providing blue-ribbon fishing in a number of Michigan rivers. Anglers from across the eastern part of the country sought the highly touted rainbow to replace the quickly dimin-

The colorful rainbow trout is the most common trout in the Smokies.

ishing brook trout. Rainbows are easily reared in hatcheries, but proved to be discontented in small streams when suitable habitat in larger waters was open to them. The wanderlust problem is of little concern to fisheries personnel in the southern Appalachian Mountains, where fish are confined to small streams and rivers (except for the existence of a few high-elevation impoundments).

Rainbow trout spawn in spring, with runs normally beginning in February. An interesting change has been observed recently in southern rainbows, with a few fish spawning in the fall. I have caught rainbows from the West Prong of the Little Pigeon in October and early November that were decked out in dark spawning hues and full of roe.

The exact date and site of the first stocking of rainbow trout in the Smokies is not known. There is some contention that landowners stocked them in Abrams Creek in 1900, though no records were kept. Today, the rainbow trout is the dominant game fish in the park, having extended its range into every stream system.

Most fish average 7 inches in length, and generally do not top 9 inches. However, an occasional 12- to 16-inch rainbow is taken. On rare days, 3- to 4-pound fish are caught. Spawning runs from impoundments (Fontana, Cheoah, and Chilhowee lakes) often bring large fish upstream for short periods of time, but this usually occurs from late December through February.

The Brown Trout (*Salmo trutta*)

The brown trout was brought to this country from Germany in 1883. Eggs shipped across the Atlantic arrived at a New York hatchery, where they were hatched and planted in local waters. Brown trout stock from Scotland arrived the following year. Fish from the German strain were called German browns or Von Behr trout, and those from Scotland were known as Loch Leven browns. For a number of years, records listed the two fish individually. Today, however, all Salmo trutta in this country are referred to as simply brown trout.

Brown trout were introduced into the Tennessee Valley in 1900. Browns in excess of 25 pounds have been caught in this region; the largest brown known to have been taken in the park was a respectable sixteen-pounder. Although browns were never stocked in the Smokies, downstream waters were stocked by both Tennessee and North Carolina fish and game agencies in the 1950s. Browns began to appear in the waters of the park in the early 1960s, and by 1977 brown trout occupied more than 50 miles of park waters.

Brown trout are primarily insect eaters, with adult mayflies being their favorite food. Halford, the famous English angling writer, wrote of the feeding habits of the brown trout: "The nymphs are the brown trout's beef, and the adult mayfly his caviar." A carnivorous creature, the brown will use everything in a stream, from tiny plankton to an occasional brother or sister. In

Brown trout are the largest-growing trout in the Smokies.

park streams, larger members of this clan are nocturnal feeders. The best time to tie into a big brown in the Smokies is at dusk or dawn, or immediately after a rain.

The brown trout can be distinguished by its generally brownish-yellow color with orange spots on the sides—although a few are sometimes a silvery tan with dark brown spots. Brown trout prefer slower water than do rainbows, but have been taken in fast waters up to 4,500 feet in elevation in park streams. These fish spawn in fall.

There is a simple reason brown trout grow larger in the waters of the Great Smoky Mountains National Park. The secret is their habitat preference compared to that of a rainbow trout. Browns are predators, more comparable to a large snake or lion, and feed only on large items. They then retire to digest their prey while remaining inactive. Rainbows are like chickadees, constantly flirting with the current for food, eating only slightly more than it takes to sustain their bulk. The energy saved by the brown trout is channeled to growth, not day-to-day survival.

The Smallmouth Bass (*Micropterus dolomieui*)

Ripping, cartwheeling surface antics are Mr. Smalljaw's calling card. This well-muscled fish's strength is overshadowed only by its courageous determination to be free, and its no-nonsense, aggressive disposition.

The smallmouth bass is a member of the Centrarchidae family of sunfish. Among the thousands who identify themselves as "bass fishermen," this fighter is their passion, the thing from which sweet dreams are made. The lower reaches of many streams in the Great Smoky Mountains National Park are prime bronzeback country. Recognizing this, the legislature made the smallmouth bass the official fish of the state of Tennessee.

The world-record smallmouth bass, which weighed 11 pounds, 15 ounces, was caught in Dale Hollow Lake in Tennessee in 1955. Actually, the fish was caught so close to the Kentucky state line that both states claim it. Being a good Volunteer State resident, however, I'll go with the home team!

The presence of smallmouth bass in the streams of the Great Smoky Mountains National Park comes as a shock to many, including a few lifelong trouters in the region. However, these marvelous game fish, as well as rock bass and even a few largemouth bass, are found in these streams. It is a bit ironic that most fly-fishermen frequenting these streams ignore the brown bass, as it is a far better fighter than any of the trout occurring here.

Part of the reason many fly-fishermen do not pursue the great smallie angling opportunities found in the park is the mistaken impression these fish can only be caught on hardware such as spinners and small crankbaits. However, nothing could be further from the truth. Smallmouth bass can be enticed to strike a variety of flies, ranging from streamers to nymphs. For the most part, all of the bass in the Smokies are most common in the lower reaches of the largest streams, such as Deep Creek and the East Prong of Little Pigeon River.

During the early years of the park, fly-fishing for smallmouth bass was almost as common as for trout. Lack of shade on many reaches of water (that are now canopied at least half of the year) resulted in prime smallmouth bass habitat. During those days, fly-fishermen used what was known then as flyrod baits. In most instances, these were scaled-down versions of proven plugs such as Heddon's Flaptail or South Bend's Bass Oreno. These bantam-sized plugs were too light to be cast with any tackle of that era other than a flyrod. Modern ultra-light tackle will cast these dainty offerings, which are now highly sought after by collectors of vintage fishing tackle.

The smallmouth bass is a member of the black bass clan, the toughest branch of the scrappy sunfish family. They resemble their larger-growing cousins, the largemouth bass, as well as the Kentucky bass. The most notable differences are in body shape and coloration. Smallies are more streamlined, and sport amber to bronze coloration. Their flanks have vertical bars, or "tiger stripes," and their eyes are reddish.

Adult smallmouth bass prefer rock- or gravel-bottomed feeding stations, which characterizes most of their habitat in the Great Smoky Mountains National Park. Three- to 5-pound smallmouth bass are trophies from these waters, while a 12-inch rock bass is a true "eye popper." Each season, a few larger bass are taken from park waters.

Crawfish, which are common to park streams, are key prey items, along with small fish such as darters and sculpins, spring lizards, insects, and other invertebrates. These fish are slightly more meat-conscious than trout, although they will take small flies.

Fly-fishing specifically for smallmouth bass is a challenging sport, but their abundance in the park makes it worthwhile. I could easily devote an entire book to this subject, as the various techniques and awesome array of fishing situations take years to master.

Experienced park smallie fly-fishermen agree that more consistent results are obtained with light tackle and relatively small baits. I like two- to four-pound-test tippets, but some fly-fishermen advocated the use of six- to eight-pound-test tippets. On occasion, it is possible to use heavier tippets, but because big bronzebacks are so easily startled, the odds are stacked against success.

Favorite smallmouth fly patters include Muddler Minnows, Joe's Hopper, large stonefly nymphs, and the Wooly Booger. Presented to the rear of pools, these fly patterns are deadly.

One reason many fly-fishing trouters fail to catch smallmouth and rock bass from the streams of the Smokies is they fail to recognize the distinctly different habitat preferences of the sunfish clan. Trout, and especially rainbows, are far more likely to be caught in modestly swift runs. Smallmouth bass shun fast water, preferring to "lay up" in the rear of pools in shaded areas.

Winter is a fine time to fish for brown bass in the park. December water temperatures and normally abundant rainfall help keep these cool-natured fish active. Streamers cannot be beat during this time, when the metabolism of the fish slows down. Streamers worked slowly over drop-offs, saddles, and bars can bring surprising results. Even during the dead of winter, smallie fishing in the streams of the park can be excellent.

Around late February, smallmouth bass begin getting active, and wander. Bottom fly-fishing rock drop-offs with streamers is an old-time tactic that still works.

March and April are exciting months for tangling with Smoky Mountain brownies. In most streams, they can be found shallow in the slow runs. Two- to 4-foot depths are not uncommon. Streamers and nymphs retrieved at a brisk pace are met by violent strikes.

Spawning action can be located along sloping gravel- or rock-bottomed areas. Plastic streamers and nymphs bounced through likely bedding cover can net an irate parent fish or two. Following the spawn, the fish spread out along rocky-bottomed areas. During the May through August period, great smallie action is available at Abrams Creek and Little River.

Some of the best smallmouth bass angling is found in Fontana Lake, an impoundment with a national reputation for producing lunker-class brownies. Using hair bugs and poppers, surface action is respectable during the spring and early summer months, especially early in the morning and late evening. Using high density lines, you can expect brisker action on subsurface offerings than at other times of the year.

Chapter 2

Smoky Mountains Angling: A Historical Overview

The story of trout fishing in the Great Smoky Mountains and the surrounding region has been largely ignored in print. Whether for sport or sustenance, fishing has long been a favorite American pursuit. Trout fishing in the crystal-clear waters of the Smokies has occupied a special place in the fabric of mountain life since before the arrival of the settlers.

The Cherokee Indians were perhaps the first people to encounter the local brook trout. The Cherokee name for these colorful little fish was "Unahnvsahti." For the Cherokee, fishing was not a recreational pastime, although it was not altogether an arduous affair.

Brook trout served as trail fare for Indian travelers crossing the rugged mountains. A favorite and very effective method of getting trout was to sprinkle a pool or two with poison made from local plants, such as the bark of the black walnut tree. After being stricken by the poison, the fish, which were usually stunned, floated to the surface and were easily gathered.

The use of a weir was another fishing technique employed by the Cherokees from capturing brook trout and other fish. A V of rocks was positioned in a stream. At the point of the V a weir was fastened down. Fish were driven downstream to be caught in the weir. This sort of effort was often a cooperative undertaking by several families or even an entire village. A community fish fry usually followed.

Early settlers arriving in the Tennessee Valley found the cloud-covered peaks mantled in the most diverse hardwood forest in the world. Preferring to carve a living out of the many rich river bottoms, most settlers bypassed the Smokies. Those who chose to live in the isolated mountains picked the rich coves and scattered bottomlands. As the population grew, some settlers moved west-

*Brook trout were unable to withstand the late nineteenth
and early twentieth century assaults of civilization.*

ward, while others moved farther up the slopes of the mountains in search of tillable land. Travel was difficult, and hard cash was scarce. The region became a backwater area in America's great western movement of the nineteenth century. It developed its own distinct culture, independent and self-reliant; the area's colorful lifestyle flourished for almost a century.

Rainbow trout were often stocked by mule-drawn sleds during the pre-park era.

Like the Cherokees, the mountain people looked upon the brook trout as a dependable source of food rather than a form of sport. Referred to as "specs" by these mountaineers, brook trout originally prospered above an elevation of 2,000 feet. The hardworking mountain people must surely have enjoyed fishing for these little fighters. Early accounts repeatedly speak of daily catches of hundreds of fish. Fishing methods such as poisoning and weirs were adopted from the Cherokees.

One favorite method commonly used in this region was known as "choking." Fish hooks were out of the reach of the economically depressed mountain people, but their resourcefulness sidestepped this problem neatly. A suitable bait was tied to a length of string and dropped into the water. When a trout would take the bait, the trick was to quickly jerk the fish out onto the bank before it had a chance to expel the bait. According to old-timers, many a meal of fresh trout came to the table as a result.

Logging in the Smokies prior to the 1880s was insignificant compared to what occurred in the next fifty-five years. The abundant forests of the southern mountains had not escaped the attention of the growing nation's appetite for wood. Large-scale logging operations descended upon the southern Appalachians near the close of the nineteenth century. The shrill sound of the narrow gauge locomotives laboring up steep grades could be heard from northern Virginia to Georgia. The Smokies, situated in the middle of this widespread activity, yielded over one billion board feet of lumber by 1935.

These cuttings devastated the land and the wildlife. The brook trout, which require unpolluted, cold water, could not cope with silt-choked streams, high water temperatures, dams, and other factors. Concerned fishermen shipped in rainbow trout in the early 1900s. The adaptable rainbow prospered. Anglers of that era contend that fishing during the first thirty years of this century was the best ever seen in these mountains. The streams were free of overhead cover. Many forms of aquatic insects prospered in the sunlight. Open glades, then common alongside many streams, were alive with grasshoppers, the favorite summer bait of that time. Trout were said to have averaged more than a pound each.

Walter Cole, a resident of Gatlinburg and now in his late nineties, was born in the Sugarland and roamed the Smokies before the arrival of the logging companies. He shared these memories with me one morning in 1980: "As I remember, I was seven years old when my father and older brother allowed me to come along when they crossed over Blanket Mountain, by the Huskey Gap Trail, to fish for trout in Little River. We packed in our cornmeal, skillet, lard, coffee, blankets, ax, and gun. We had our crop laid in, with harvesting time still a ways off. In those days, anybody could just go up in the mountains, build a shelter, and stay as long as they wanted, huntin' and fishin'.

"The logging people hadn't come yet, and the creeks were swarming with speckle trouts, thick as gnats. It was always dark as sundown, fishin' for them, with the big hemlocks and poplars shading out the light. It was easy to catch all the 10- to 14-inch fish you wanted then. I've even caught a few that were a tad longer than 16 inches.

"We set up camp and gathered enough stickbait to last all day, then cut us a good birch sapling for a fishin' pole. We started up the creek, stringing our catch on a stick till it wouldn't hold another fish. We set it down in a deep pool to keep it cool, moving on upstream doing the same until we had caught all we wanted. On the way back to camp, we collected the hidden fish, fried them whole in hot grease, and ate them with nothin' except cornbread. That was the best eatin' I ever had. We would do that every summer, sometimes staying for weeks living on fish and game we'd sometimes shoot. Come frost, we'd be sure to be home to get in the corn and cut wood."

Cole later went to work for the Little River Logging Company, where he did a bit of everything. He recalled the riotous living in the Elkmont camp, where moonshine, gambling, fast women, and fishing were as much a part of living as sawdust and splinters.

"I was there when the first rainbow trout came into camp from Michigan. They raised them up in a run next to Little River. When they were ready to release them in the creeks, they turned half of them loose in Little River, and hauled the others over Huskey Gap, by a mule-pulled wagon, in rain barrels, to the West Prong of the Little Pigeon. I believe the year was 1911. The fishery people have been trying to figure out what has driven the "specs" off. I can tell you in one word—rainbow. The brook trout's time has passed. Someday I figure the rainbow may have to give way to the brown trout, just the same way."

During these years, the Smokies began to attract the attention of serious anglers. Some were sport fishermen whose lines were tipped with a feathery fly; others preferred to cast dynamite into a pool. The American angling scene, which during the late 1980s had seen the introduction of brightly-colored flies for trout, was undergoing a change of its own during these times. An angler from New York, Theodore Gordon, was experimenting with a new technique for taking trout. Correspondence between Gordon and F. M. Halford, an Englishman dubbed the "father of dry fly-fishing," led to Halford's sending Gordon a sample of English dry flies. From this beginning, the sport of dry fly-fishing spread from Gordon's home waters in the Catskills down the Appalachian range. In the southern Appalachians, however, it was not nearly as quickly embraced as in many other regions.

Most early anglers of the South used the old "buggy whip" style rods, or a simple cane pole. The buggy whip rods were sometimes homemade from such materials as ash, hickory, or cherry. Hair from the tail of a stallion or gelding was used to make fishing line. (Many experienced fishermen shunned the use of hair from a mare or filly because it was believed that contact with urine weakened the strength of the hairs.)

Most Appalachian trout fishermen lacked the funds to purchase the five-dollar Charles F. Orvis flyrods, or even the one-dollar bamboo rods pictured in the large mail-order catalogs. There was at least one local rod building, located in Pigeon Forge. The Ramsey Rods, built completely from scratch, lacked the exquisite craftsmanship of those from the shops in the East; yet they exhibited a fine feel and were affordable. Those that remain today are treasured by their owners.

Each little community had its own group of devoted hunters and anglers. They spent an enormous amount of time hunting bear or raccoon, and fishing. Having a reputation for being in the mountains at all hours was also useful to those making moonshine. The phrase "going fishing" often implied one was going to brew "corn squeezins." I sometimes wonder if trout, which are fond of sweet corn, did not develop this taste during the days of moonshine making, when mash was commonly dumped in the streams!

Trout fishing gradually became a form of recreation. The use of bait slowly gave way to the use of artificials. In those days, each streamshed of the Smokies had a few men who worked as guides for fishing, hiking, or hunting, as the era of the traveling hunter/fisherman was becoming popular nationwide.

Robert S. Masonin, in his now out-of-print book, *The Lure of the Smokies*, published in 1927, devoted several pages to fishing in the Smoky Mountains. He listed the names of guides who were available for hire, flies that were most effective, and comments from a number of long-time anglers of the region.

Matt Whittle, a Gatlinburg horticulturist by trade, fished the streams of the Smokies all his life, and was perhaps the best-known angler on the Tennessee side of the mountains. Dubbed the "Izaak Walton" of the Smokies, Whittle understood the habits of his quarry as few have. Going against the common belief of his day that indicated matching the hatch when fishing with flies, Whittle felt it was of no real importance what kind of fly you used, but how you fished with what you were using, and how the fish were feeding. Whittle often left his shrubbery business to guide "Yankee" fishermen up the streams of the Smokies. Well-known angler George LeBranche is said to have been among those who accompanied Whittle into the Smokies.

The Hazel Creek area was one of the most developed regions of the Smokies prior to the formation of the National Park. It was also the stomping ground of Colonel Calhoun and the well-known Hazel Creek Club. From their lodge, which was located on Hazel Creek near the present-day Calhoun back country campsite, members hunted boar, bear, and deer during the winter, and fished for trout during the summer. Tales of the exploits of these rough-and-ready men and their favorite hounds are still the subject of lively discussions among locals.

One of the most famous duos of the mountains were two North Carolina men named Samuel Hunnicutt and Mark Cathey. Natives

*During World War II, catches such as this are
said to have been common in the Smokies.*

of the Bryson City/Deep Creek area, they were said to have been
inseparable companions from the turn of the century through the
1920s. Deep Creek, which they considered the best fishing in the
country, was a favorite haunt of both. Cathey occasionally guided
fishermen into the Smokies. He accompanied Horace Kephart up
Deep Creek on a number of Kephart's many trips. Kephart, aside
from being one of the earliest outdoor scribes to give accounts of
the Smokies and an outspoken advocate for the formation of the
national park, was fond of trout fishing in these mountains.
Cathey took considerable satisfaction in allowing his guest to
watch him bewitch trout using his "dance of the fly." Using a long
cane pole, he would dabble the fly over the water in a figure eight,
enticing even the most wary and sullen trout into a vicious strike.

Hunnicutt and Cathey would spend weeks at a time on the upper
reaches of Deep Creek. An amusing tale concerning one of their trips
tells of the two leaving camp one morning at the forks of the Left
Prong and the mainstream of Deep Creek. Cathey was to fish the Left
Prong until supper, and Hunnicutt the Right Prong. Hunnicutt
found the fish less than cooperative, and returned to camp
empty-handed. Cathey had not yet made it back, so after waiting for

a while, Hunnicutt decided to try his hand up the Left Prong and meet Cathey on his return trip. He'd fished approximately 300 yards of the creek, creeling eleven nice trout along the way, when he rounded a bend and saw Cathey, who had ninety trout strung over his shoulder. Hunnicutt asked Cathey if he was mad about his coming to meet him. Cathey's reply was short and rather stern, as he eyed the eleven fish at Hunnicutt's side: "No, but had you not come to meet me, I would have had a hundred trout when I reached camp."

Carl Standing Deer of the Qualla Reservation was perhaps the best-known sport angler among the Cherokees during the early years of the park. Standing Deer, whose greatest call to fame rested on his deadly aim with his hand-built bow, proudly referred to himself as the grandson of Suyetta, the revered Cherokee storyteller. Standing Deer was a dyed-in-the-wool traditionalist, who used horsehair lines after gut and even nylon lines were available, and scorned flies, preferring stickbait and wasp larvae. Standing Deer considered Deep Creek to have the finest fishing in the Smokies, and was occasionally available as a guide.

After the national park was formed, the fishing changed. Gradually, bait fishing became illegal in all park waters. Creel and size limits were imposed. Auto access to many streams became a thing of the past. With the building of Fontana Dam, the park grew, as the Tennessee Valley Authority turned over much of the land it had acquired from residents who would have been isolated as a result of the impounding of the Little Tennessee River. The power from Fontana Dam was funneled into the nation's atomic research center at Oak Ridge. The Smokies were the site of some secret road-building practice for the Army Corps of Engineers and of other experiments for the military.

Until 1947 the streams of the Smokies were annually restocked with large numbers of both brook and rainbow trout, in an effort to provide park visitors with "quality" fishing. Rearing stations were operated at the Chimneys, Tremont, Cades Cove, and on Kephart's Prong. Today, the Smokies offer fine sport fishing for rainbow and brown trout. Fishing for brook trout was sharply curtailed in 1975, when a large number of brook trout streams were closed to all fishing, and it then became illegal to kill a brook trout.

This area is rich in tradition and fishing tales. When tramping down the banks of these streams, it is always interesting to wonder what happened along these trails in previous years.

Chapter 3

About Those Creeks

There is no such thing as a typical pool, run, or glide in the Great Smoky Mountains National Park, much less a typical stream. One of the truly great things about fly-fishing here is the virtually infinite variety of angling challenges and opportunities found among the 733 miles of streams in the national park. Frankly, that variety has astonished every one of the hundreds of anglers I have guided on fly-fishing trips over the last quarter of a century.

Streams in the Great Smoky Mountains National Park can be broken down into five categories, with single streams often containing all categories as they progress from their headwaters to their ending points, or where they leave the park. The five are small rivers, medium-size low gradient streams, medium-size high gradient streams, small high gradient streams, and "brush" creeks.

Small rivers, or Class I waters as they are noted in this book, include the lower reaches of the Oconaluftee River, Little River, and Abrams Creek. These differ dramatically from headwater rills. Gradient and flow volume are the key differences, although as a rule the farther downstream the pH of a stream is measured, the higher it is, thus the more fertile it becomes.

Small river-like streams in the Great Smoky Mountains National Park share several common characteristics. They are wide in many places; these flows spread out shallowly in areas up to 200 feet wide over river slicks and bedrock. These spots are dotted with pocket waters that usually hold trout throughout the year. These streams also hold the largest percentage of long, slow pools with bottoms of fine gravel and sand that appear to be custom-made for fly-fishing the last hour of the day, when duns are most common. These waters also boast a sprinkling of plunge pools, with examples of the most extreme being Abrams Falls and the Sinks on the Little River. Another characteristic of the park's small rivers is the trees found along each side of these flows rarely meet to form a complete canopy over the stream.

A significant portion of the largest trout and bass found in the Great Smoky Mountains National Park populate these small river reaches. This is usually because these streams provide larger trout with more "elbow room," and they also offer a greater quantity and variety of forage than smaller, higher elevation streams.

These large streams also provide fly-fishermen with the greatest opportunities to use a variety of techniques to catch trout and bass. Hundred-foot casts or longer are possible on some stretches and pools, although to be honest, the short line method of fishing is usually more effective than "gold medal-style" distance casting.

The medium-size low gradient stream classification, or Class II waters, covers the lower reaches of streams such as Eagle Creek, Hurricane Creek, or Panther Creek. These streams resemble scaled-down versions of the previously mentioned small rivers. They average 14 to 30 feet wide, and more often than not the over-story of trees meets over the creeks to form a shading canopy during summer. Medium-size low gradient streams usually have pH levels very comparable to those of the low elevation small rivers. The average pH in these waters is 7.2 to 7.8. These streams typically host outstanding populations of caddis flies and mayflies, but are not the best producers of stoneflies.

Medium-size, low gradient streams offer their best fly-fishing for trout in winter and spring. These streams tend to warm during the summer, and early autumn trout will migrate upstream, where higher elevations provide cooler habitat and the faster flow increases the level of dissolved oxygen. During hot weather, though, many of these streams offer outstanding, but largely over-looked, opportunities to catch smallmouth bass on a flyrod by using hair bugs.

In the Great Smoky Mountains National Park, medium-size, high gradient streams, or Class III waters, comprise a significant portion of my favorite fly-fishing waters. This type can be in the upper reaches of the two previously noted classifications of water, or it can be a major watershed such as Big Creek. In terms of size, these streams are nearly identical to the medium-size, low gradient streams, although it is far more common for these waters to constrict to a mere few feet when they wash between large boulders. One of the biggest differences fly-fishermen will note is the high rate of flow in these waters, which often feature staircase-like series of plunge pools connected by swift, shallow runs that occasionally terminate in large, deep pools.

Class III waters usually have heavy overstory canopies. More often than not, these streams tumble rapidly over massive "greybacks" (a nickname given to stream boulders by the locals) as they rush down the steep sides of the Smoky Mountains. The best time to fly-fish many of these waters is from late spring through early autumn, when many trout migrate upstream to take advantage of the cooler temperatures and the higher levels of dissolved oxygen the rushing ripples and cascades inject into the water.

Average pH levels on medium-size, high gradient streams vary considerably, from 6.8 to 7.4 (7.0 is neutral) on some streams, to a low 6.0 to 6.4 on a few others. In the Great Smoky Mountains National Park, these streams are fairly decent producers of prime trout foods such as mayflies, caddis flies, and stoneflies. Some of the best hatches of the eastern salmonfly (Pternarcys), the largest stonefly found in park waters, and the giant golden stonefly (Aconeuria) occur on these waters. Mayflies are also common in these waters, especially those such as the Epeorus (which includes the quill gordon), which demand unpolluted, highly oxygenated water to thrive.

Fishing quality is good to excellent on virtually all of these streams. Rainbow are the primary quarry found here, but large brown trout often rule large pools, and brook trout are not as rare in some waters as many might have you believe. My all-time favorite method of fly-fishing streams in the Great Smoky Mountains National Park, that is, standing in a downstream plunge pool and fishing the pool immediately above it at eye level, can be practiced with the consistency of daily sunrises on many stretches of the medium-size, high gradient streams.

Small, high gradient, or Class IV streams, are scaled-down versions of the Class III flows. Examples of this type of water are Walker Prong, Ramsey Fork, and the upper reaches of Eagle Creek. Class IV streams include the upper reaches of the majority of the primary streams noted in this guidebook. Primary differences include less flow volume, and in many instances lower pH levels, which result in lower fertility. The latter translates to fewer pounds of trout per surface.

With the exception of the deep plunge pools that are found periodically along these streams, the depth of the water is rarely more than knee deep. Stream widths vary from 4 to 20 feet. Flow rates are "super charged," with long slow pools rarely being found, although they do occur. Quarries in these streams vary from the primary species, the rainbow trout, followed by the brook trout as well as a few brown trout.

Small, high gradient streams offer trout cool sanctuary during hot weather, but this is also when they are at their lowest flow volume. These waters can be difficult to fish when flow levels are low, as trout tend to stack up in placid pools that not only require precision casting under often difficult-to-negotiate, dense forest canopies, but also demand delicate presentation. Spring is a great time to fly-fish these waters. Another outstanding time to "go high" is during the summer, when rainy weather has made downstream reaches in the park difficult to fly-fish. Rain runoff occurs quickly in the Smokies, and the first water to hit ideal flow levels is always the headwater streams.

Fly-fishing tactics for small, high gradient streams are similar to those noted for Class III streams. Like many other fly-fishermen, I like to downsize my tackle for these waters, usually opting to use a 6.5-foot Orvis Flea designed to cast a 2-weight fly line. A trick for catching trout from these waters during times of low flow, which was taught to me by a friend from Waynesville, North Carolina, is to use boulders along and in the stream to aid in fly presentation. Picture a run of water emptying into a pool as quietly as if you were pouring tea from a pitcher. Dropping a fly delicately enough to avoid spooking trout located near the entering water is tough. However, if you cast so your fly line either never enters the water (that is, it lands on streamside gravel and rocks), you will draw a strike. The same principle can be used on other slow flows, where midstream boulders and rocks can be used for temporarily "parking" fly line, while upstream only the leader, or even just the tippet, comes down on the pool.

The brush stream classification, or Class V category in this book, actually is a relatively diminutive group of streams few users of this guidebook are ever likely to fly-fish or find interesting. On the other hand, insofar as I have always been a "small creek freak," I am compelled to include them. These are the smallest fishable (and in some instances semi-fishable) flows in the Great Smoky Mountains National Park. At high elevations, many of these waters have been closed to fishing since the brook moratorium of 1975.

Size and canopy are the biggest differences separating brush creeks from Class IV and III streams. In most instances, brush creeks are slightly to significantly smaller than the Class IV waters found in the park. Examples of brush creeks include the upper reaches of Little Cataloochee Creek, Beetree Creek (a tributary of Deep Creek) and Bee Gum Branch (a tributary of Forney Creek). Average widths are 2 to 10 feet. As the name implies, brush creeks are usually heavily overgrown on at least enough of their courses to make travel along the streambed a taxing adventure even to the stoutest souls.

This is not to imply portions, often even large reaches, are not brushed over with steel-tough tangles of rhododendron and laurel. Plunge pools, and occasionally large trout, are the secrets these trickles can reveal to those willing to fight the streamside greenery.

Rainbow and brook trout are the primary quarries on these waters. Early spring and during the summer after or during rain are the only truly good times to make trips to any of these waters. Fly-fishing is tough on all but the most open sections of a brush creek. Tactics are largely the same as outlined for Class III and V waters. One interesting variation is dabbling, which is often more effective when done downstream. The trick is to allow just enough tippet to extend from the tip of your rod to permit you to negotiate getting a fly into a pool, which many times has only a few inches of clearance between the surface and the top of the overhead bushes. Sure, you will get a strike doing this, that is the easy part. What takes practice is setting the hook and, once you have accomplished that, working your catch out of the hole without getting everything tangled in the brush.

Chapter 4

Where To Find Fish
and Why

Angling for Smokies trout is not limited to expert fishermen. Trout can be caught on a two-dollar cane pole, or on a four-hundred-dollar graphite flyrod. Fine fishing tackle is a joy to use, but by no means is it a prerequisite for success. The name of the game is having fun.

Several important bits of information will aid in catching trout. Anglers increase their chances if they knows where their quarry prefers to "hang out," and what morsels are most tempting to its palate. Other important keys to success include mastering a stealthy approach to the stream, and being able to place your offering in a spot where it will not alarm the fish.

Each of the three trout of the Smokies tends to occupy slightly different water when feeding, although any one species may occasionally be in any given spot. Trout in the wild have established feeding spots, or stations, where they position themselves to await food coming down with the current. Size and aggressiveness determine how good a feeding spot a trout is able to defend and keep.

Understanding where trout position themselves in the stream is one of the most important bits of knowledge an angler can possess. When surveying a pool or stretch of pocket water for likely fish-holding spots, remember a trout must have cover that shields it from the current, and offers at least limited shelter during times of danger. A typical pool starts with a noisy waterfall. The water rushes over smooth, gray boulders, falling into a carved-out plunge pool. Current-loving rainbow trout are right at home in the swift waters of the plunge pool. Large rainbow trout often station themselves at the base of the falls, while smaller members of the clan will gather around the perimeter of the pool, or in the pool's main channel. From the depths of the plunge pool, the flow

*Nearly all of the brook trout in the Great Smokies
are found in small streams like this.*

of the stream moves on to the tail of the pool, where the average
depth becomes more shallow. It is here you will often find the
secretive brown trout. His favorite lairs are near solitary rocks or
submerged tree roots alongside the bank. These fish, particularly
the large fellows, often shun feeding during the day, preferring to
chase minnows at night. Brook trout favor much the same sort of
habitat as the brown trout, though the brookie does not shy away
from a sunlit meal. Pocket water, so common to the park, can be
treated like a miniature pool.

Brown trout occupy slower water.

Where fish are located is important, but knowing their feeding habits is of equal importance. The trout of the park are best termed "opportunistic feeders." The streams of the Smokies and the surrounding mountains are poor producers of food; they are acidic and carry only a limited amount of nutrients (Abrams Creek is the only notable exception). While by no means devoid

*Bigger rainbow trout are more common in the lower
reaches of streams where there is more "elbow room."*

of aquatic insects, local streams do not support the massive concentrations of the spring-run limestone creeks of Pennsylvania, or
Hampshire, England. A typical trout will, in the course of a few

hours, consume a combination of mayflies, caddis flies, stoneflies, midges, and a terrestrial or two. Close examination of their stomach contents will reveal dominant feeding on the most abundant food, but along with that particular food, a few other tidbits will usually be present. During the late winter and very early spring, Smokies trout feed primarily on the nymphs.

Spring is a time of brisk activity in and on the streams. As the season progresses, the weather becomes milder, warming the water. Insect emergence becomes more common, along with surface feeding by trout. Such activity peaks by late spring, about the only time local trout can afford to be selective, so fly selection should be considered. Terrestrials quickly become important to the diet of the trout, even in spring.

Summer fishing action is often slow. The remaining insect hatches are small and sporadic. Streams suffer from the seasonal dry weather, often running at little more than a trickle, compared to a couple of months earlier. Water temperatures rise, causing many trout to seek deep, cool havens and to feed at night. Successful anglers often use terrestrial insect imitations, such as grasshoppers, ants, jassids (or leafhoppers), beetles, caterpillars, and bees.

Fall is an exciting time. The scenery surrounding the streams is at its best. Trees and shrubs are decked out in their brightest yellows, flame reds, spectacular oranges, and regal golds. Trout seem to sense the coming winter, and feed with uncharacteristic abandon. Terrestrials are still the cornerstone of their diets, although often overlooked are some interesting hatches of caddis flies. During late fall, growing nymphs and larvae take on increasing dietary importance.

The cold winter months cause trout to becoming torpid and staying close to the bottom. The cold water slows down fish's metabolism, reducing the amount of food needed to survive. Anglers feeling the urge to fish during the winter will be pleased to learn that on the mild days, trout move into the sunny areas and do a modest amount of feeding.

Armed with an understanding of where the trout are and what their food preferences are, anglers can use their knowledge on the stream. The importance of a quiet approach and accurate presentation of the chosen lure or fly cannot be overemphasized. Try not to hurry. Stand back for a minute to observe and plan a strategy.

*Wading boots with felt soles, or removeable gripper chains,
are recommended when wading these streams.*

The fish are usually facing upstream, into the current. Most experienced Smoky Mountains trout fishermen prefer to fish upstream, thus coming up behind their quarry. Exceptions to this would be in times of high or cloudy water. Unless you are an expert caster, chances are you will not place every cast in the desired spot, but if you can hit the right spot with the right offering often enough, you will catch fish.

One question I am often asked, "What is the best way to fish the streams of the park—fly-fishing, spinners, or what?" The simplest and least expensive way to have a productive day on one of the creeks of the Smokies is to incorporate the use of a simple cane pole. Use of cane poles was widespread in the Smokies prior to World War II, and it is still fairly common to encounter an old fisherman from Bryson City or Cosby fishing with a 10- to 14-foot cane pole. The mountain folk are deadly with these.

Besides being very effective, cane poles are one of the least expensive routes you can take. An out-of-state visitor who forgets his fishing gear and wants to try his luck in park waters can purchase a pole, a spool of four-pound test line, a half-dozen flies, and a fishing permit for less than fifteen dollars.

A cane pole enables you to stand back from the area where the fly is dropped. Tactics employed when using a cane pole are almost the same as those used when fly-fishing, and the basics are the same for a wet fly, dry fly, or a nymph. Attempt to drop the fly along the edges of waterfalls, allowing the current to carry it to the end of the pool or run. If a strike does not occur the first time, and you feel there is a fish in the area, repeat the drift in a slightly different section of the pool. Keep a tight line the entire time your fly is in or on the water, as a lightning-fast strike can occur at any point.

Fly-fishermen may be the classic attention-getters of the trout streams, but the spinner fishermen account for more trophy trout. Chasing after tiny insects might satisfy smaller fish, but a large fish may have to expend more energy on an insect than can be derived from its consumption. For this reason, large trout depend on minnows, crayfish, and even smaller trout for their daily fare.

Chapter 5

Casting Tactics and Tips

One of the first things many fly fishermen notice when casting in the streams of the Great Smoky Mountains National Park is it rarely is what they expected before they tried. Even accomplished fly casters sometimes experience difficulty adjusting to the low overhead canopies and swift currents of these streams. Classic casting, where the line goes above the head of the caster on the backcast, can be impossible to accomplish on these waters. Personally, I have never liked the surface disturbance roll back-casting creates, so I rarely do or recommend this for these streams.

Fly-fishermen find that the biggest obstacle to ideal fishing conditions is the lack of casting room, plus problems with drag. You will find yourself doing a good deal of sidearm casting, especially on some of the small streams. Plan to lose a few flies while angling these canopied waters.

While I do not tout myself as an expert fly-fisherman, I do catch trout and bass from these streams using these techniques. One thing I have learned over the years from fly-fishing here is that what is behind you is just as important as what lies ahead. By this, I am referring to the infernal trees and limbs the National Park Service has shown little inclination to trim to improve my casting ease. It usually happens when I walk up on an extremely inviting run, where I know an eager-to-strike trout is waiting for my challenge. For the last fifty casts I have looked behind me, working my backcast through "keyhole" size openings in the streamside greenery. (This is an art form that those who fly-fish in these streams eventually master.) However, in the excitement of coming up on the best run of the day, I forget to check my backcast. Whammo!—my last No.14 Adams takes up permanent residence 16 feet up a hemlock. Even by extending the butt of my flyrod into the tree to use the reel as a hook, I am out of luck.

Unorthodox casting techniques are the rule rather than the exception on all but the largest waters in the Great Smoky Mountains National Park. Many times, presenting a fly under a limb hanging a foot above the surface can only be accomplished by sidearm casting. This easy-to-master technique requires two things—knowing what is behind you and deadly casting accuracy. Under these conditions, there is no room for error.

Next to casting difficulties in tight conditions, drag problems are the next thing that surprises newcomers to these waters. The degree of problem drag represents will depend on the sort of water you are attempting to challenge. If you cast to water that has few crosscurrents, or limit yourself to extremely short casts, drag will be minimal. If you prefer to make long casts across broken pocket water, or exposed rocks, you will be forced to mend your line constantly. Proficient fly-casters who attempt long shots into distant feeding lanes across such barriers and who have experience with an ever-constant drag will catch considerably more fish. When concentrating your efforts on short, easy casts, you often risk getting close enough to the fish to alert them to your presence.

Several things facilitate dealing with the fast, swirling currents found on many runs in the streams of the Great Smoky Mountains National Park. The instant your fly is on the water, begin mending line. By holding the tip of your flyrod aloft, you can get more line off the water, thus less line is exposed to the current. The result usually is less drag. A leader that is at least 9 to 10 feet long also can reduce the headaches nearly every fly fisherman experiences dealing with drag on these waters.

Picking an ideal flyrod for the streams of the Smokies is a job comparable to picking the ideal wine. Long flyrods (9 to 9.5 feet) have been the choice of a number of highly successful, long-time patrons of the region; but an almost equal number of noted fly fishermen prefer extremely short flyrods (6 to 6.5 feet).

Those favoring the long rod say the added length allows them to keep more line off the water, this helping to eliminate drag. Greater casting accuracy is also cited as a plus for the long rod. The school which favors short rods cites the use of light lines (No.3 to No.4) and maneuverability on the stream as solid advantages. The short rod is easy to work on small streams, where overhead growth can hinder casting.

Regardless of your choice in the length of your flyrod, it should be of good quality. For dry fly fishing, flyrods should be engineered to cast fly lines in the 2 to 4 weight class. Weight forward lines are recommended on these waters where you are not always afforded the luxury of traditional, power building casts. When fly-fishing using streamers, wet flies, or nymphs, heavier fly lines in the 5 to 8 weight class work well on these waters. My personal flyrod is a Redmont, designed to cast 4 weight line. It is light and responsive, yet extremely powerful. Costing half the price of other flyrods of its caliber, the Redmont comes with a lifetime guarantee.

Fly reel choices for these waters are of the single-action variety. Most modern single-action fly reels, such as those made by Scientific Angler or Orvis, have acceptable drag systems, something most anglers here will never use. More important than a good drag in a fly reel is having a reel that balances well with the flyrod.

During the winter months waders are necessary, although I did not know this until I was in my mid-twenties, when a man told me cold water wet wading caused arthritis. Neoprene waders in the 3-millimeter range are perfect for not only keeping you warm and dry, but also for helping to cushion the occasional falls you certainly will take in these waters. Neoprene may be the greatest thing to happen to cold water wading since humans walked upright, but these spongy wonders do have their drawbacks. Walking any distance in neoprene waders is akin to sitting in a sauna. For big guys such as myself, putting on and taking off neoprene waders gives one a new appreciation for what women go through with pantyhose.

During warmer weather, micro-thin waders such as those offered by Red Ball, or just wading wet (my personal favorite) will suffice. From about the middle of May through early October, my standard wading apparel includes shorts, wool socks, and felt-soled wading boots. Wading boots with felt soles, spikes, felt soles with spikes, or slip-on chains are essential for safe wading in the slippery-bottomed streams of the Great Smoky Mountains National Park.

Chapter 6

Weather, Seasons, and Other Factors

Few places in the United States frequented by fly-fishermen are more at the mercy of the seasons and weather than the streams of the Great Smoky Mountains National Park. Understanding how weather and the seasons affect trout behavior in these waters can appreciably enhance your enjoyment of angling there, as well as up your odds for success.

Winter Fly-fishing

Winter fishing is relatively new to the streams of the Great Smoky Mountains National Park. Until the mid-1970s, most of these streams were closed to all angling between late October and mid-April. These practice was a carry-over from the old fishery management days, when it was believed that wading streams during the winter damaged the trout eggs resting in shallow gravel beds located in the tails of swift runs. Prior to the 1970s, only the West Prong of the Little Pigeon, the Little, and the Oconoluftee rivers were open to year-round angling.

Abolishment of closed fishing seasons in the Great Smoky Mountains National Park was, until recently, largely enjoyed by a small cadre of local anglers. Unlike trout streams found farther north in the Appalachian Mountains, the flows in this park rarely ice over, especially in their lower reaches. During periods of warm weather, which are relatively common to winters in the region, exceptionally good fly-fishing, even with dry flies, is the rule rather than the exception.

Aquatic insects hatch all winter, but especially when the mercury climbs above forty-seven degrees Fahrenheit. This is true even in headwater brook trout streams. The trout found in these waters are not as active during the winter as they are at other times of the year, but their predictable opportunistic feeding habits can

Winter fishing is outstanding most of the time in the Smokies.

still be very effectively used by fly-fishermen. In fact, some of the biggest brown and rainbow trout caught by flyrodders are landed at this time.

Winter fly-fishing for trout can be notoriously inconsistent, while casting for smallmouth bass is a little more predictable. Weather is the key to success. My favorite days are bluebird, low wind, mild temperature days, particularly when they are preceded by two days when the temperature gradually warmed and it did not rain. This is largely a personal preference, as is my liking for days when the weather is nice, occasionally reaching sixty to eighty degrees Fahrenheit by mid-afternoon. Such weather guarantees flies will be in the air and trout will not only be feeding in the runs, but also lounging in the tails of long, slow pools. However, it is not the only time trout and bass can be caught in large numbers and size during winter.

Approaching cold front days, those days when the sky is a Confederate gray and menacing, often offer the best winter fishing of the year. Frankly, I do not believe anyone understands precisely what is about an approaching cold front and the resulting barometric changes that brings out feeding binges in Mother Nature's world. All I know is it happens to everything from songbirds and white-tailed deer, to trout and bass. I recall fishing at Smokemont once when an ice storm warning had been issued. By noon, the temperature was near sixty degrees Fahrenheit, and by three o'clock it was spitting snow and sleet.

The fishing, though, was phenomenal that afternoon, akin to dabbling salmon eggs in a hatchery run full of starving trout. I nearly got stranded in the mountains because of making "one last cast" too many times that day. By the time I could tear myself away, the roads had become virtually impassable, but I had taken three brown trout over 18 inches, and more 10- to 12-inch rainbows than I had seen in the preceding spring and summer months combined.

That is but one example of the fine winter angling I have enjoyed over the last three decades of fly-fishing in the Great Smoky Mountains National Park. Fly-fishing these streams during approaching cold fronts can be a bit hairy at times, but the pay-off is often worth taking a chance.

One of the nicest aspects of fly-fishing during winter in the Great Smoky Mountains National Park is that the best fishing occurs during what is usually the most pleasant time of the day—late morning through mid-afternoon. For the most part this is when air temperatures are warmest, which triggers fly hatches, which in turn accelerates feeding by trout and bass. As always, exceptions do occur. Most notably this relates to larger trout, especially browns. These fish remain remarkably nocturnal even during the cold weather months. Late evening and early morning fly-fishing for big trout by using a Muddler Minnow, Spuddler, or other streamer can be extremely effective, as is drifting large stonefly nymphs through long, slow runs. However, at this time of the year, when planning your fishing trips to the park, you can sleep late, get home in time for supper, and still cash in on the peak fishing hours.

Another quirk that characterizes big trout during winter in the national park is this is when mature rainbow and brown trout accomplish most of their spawning. While it is true that spawning occurs in autumn, it peaks between early February and the last full moon period in March. Spawning trout in larger streams move to headwater areas, where they can be caught. The most interesting spawning action, though, is found upstream from the mouth of the streams which empty into the lakes bordering the southern edge of the park. Large trout from the lakes make their way upstream, often in surprisingly large numbers, where they spawn in small- to medium-size feeder streams. During its peak, this spawning run at Abrams Creek upstream from Chilhowee Lake offers fishing akin to that found in Alaska. This is the only time I recommend flies that mimic roe.

Just as there are best times, there are also times when you are better off tying flies in front of a warm fire than making a trip to these waters. When snow is falling, these trout and bass are not particularly difficult to entice to strike a dry fly or a nymph. However, when water from melting snow is entering these streams, it negatively affects trout and bass. Much the same is true of when cold rain is falling in the mountains. During winter, trees and other plant life in the Smokies do not use rainfall to nearly the same degree as in spring and summer. The net result is typically a greater flow volume in the streams than at other times. During and following rainy weather, park streams, even the high-elevation rivulets, are often too high to effectively fish, short of using a lead line and heavily-weighted nymphs.

Tactics for catching winter trout are simple. The tails of pools often hold more actively feeding trout now than at most other times of the year. Deep ripples also harbor rainbow trout in large numbers, while brookies and brown trout will be found lurking under deadfalls, undercut banks, and the side areas of large- to medium-sized pools. These fish are not as active now as during most other times of the year, but they certainly can be caught almost anytime with varying degrees of success.

Dark fly patterns are the norm, with No.14 to No.16 being the most common. (See the chapters on flies and fly patterns for more information.) Clad in neoprene waders, anglers can withstand the cold water temperatures throughout the day. (I personally wish to thank whoever developed these fantastic waders.) It is often possible to fly-fish these waters with only a wool shirt above the waist, if you top it with a lightweight jacket or shirt featuring W. L. Gore's Windstopper fabric.

Spring Fly-fishing

Any fly-fisherman unable to have a great time on the streams of the Great Smoky Mountains National Park during March, April, and May probably needs to have a new leisure-time activity. If there is a better place in the southern Appalachian highlands for fly-fishermen to be in spring, I have yet to discover it during my travels. However, spring does not occur uniformly throughout the Great Smoky Mountains National Park.

The first signs of spring are evident at the lowest elevations, such as the mouth of Abrams Creek, and the lower reaches of the Cataloochee Valley. The changing of the season progresses up the slopes of the mountains in stages, culminating at the crests just above the starting points of the headwater rills. First-time visitors to the park in mid-May see lush, green foliage at the lower elevations near the Sugarlands Park Headquarters; after driving for ten minutes, they are often shocked to discover the same species of trees still budding at Newfound Gap.

Spring progresses in the streams of the park in much the same manner, which is why in my first fishing guide books to these waters, I did not include my detailed fly emergence data. A single stream such as the West Prong of the Little Pigeon River could, in the course of a single day in mid-May, experience fly hatches that resemble early spring hatches at the 4,000-foot elevation, and early summer hatches at the 1,500-foot elevation. This, coupled with the incredible diversity of the benthic macroinvertebrate community found in the streams of the Great Smoky Mountains National Park and the highly opportunistic feeding habits of these trout and bass, makes in-depth fly hatch emergence information of limited value. Nevertheless, many fly-fishermen asked for the information, so it is in this volume.

Extended periods of rainfall typically occur during spring, and as you might expect, flow levels are strong, exceeded only in overall volume by those of winter. Actually, it is not terribly uncommon for dry spells to occur at this time, which can shrink some streams back to levels most anglers familiar with these waters normally associate with the dog days of summer. However, for the most part, fly-fishermen are more likely to encounter optimal flow levels at these streams during spring than at any other time of the year. The benefit of good flow levels is more trout are likely to be found in the feeding lanes, and as a result, they have only a short time to examine approaching flies.

Day-long good fishing is a hallmark of spring fly-fishing for trout and smallmouth bass, although your odds of catching a big fish are better very early in the morning and late in the afternoon. The last thing you want to do is cancel a fishing trip on those dreary, overcast days, or even those days when a drizzle, not a steady rain, dominates the weather. Some of the best spring fly-fishing I have enjoyed over the last twenty-five years occurred on those ugly days when it was not really raining, but the air was permeated with half mist and half rain.

Most experienced Smoky Mountain fly-fishermen split their spring casting efforts between nymphs/wet flies and dry flies, with a few being astute enough to realize the deadly effectiveness of big streamers such as the Muddler Minnow and Spuddler (sizes No.4 to No.8). (Personally, at this time I enjoy great success casting a dry fly in conjunction with a nymph dropper.)

This is the time of year most knowledgeable fly-fishermen carry the greatest variety of fly patterns. Spring is a transitional time, when nymphs and adult aquatic insects not only become more abundant, but they also become larger and lighter in color. The "single to ten fly" anglers I know who, for the most part rely on one pattern, that is, the Adams, carry this single pattern in three to six color variations, ranging from very light gray body with light hackle, to a medium gray body with brown hackle, to an almost black body with dark gray hackle. At the very least, your fly box should contain a good selection of mayfly and caddis fly adults, ranging in color from relatively dark to light.

Spring is a great time to drift nymphs through dark runs and shallow glides. Again, your fly boxes should contain a variety. Caddis fly pupa patterns and mayfly and stonefly nymph patterns should reflect diversity (see the charts in "Stream Insects and Feathery Deceivers," Chapter 7), particularly in size and color. If you remember anything in this book about the aquatic insects found in the streams of the Great Smoky Mountains National Park, remember that as winter gives way to spring, the flies and nymphs undergo a transition from black, dark brown, and gray to light gray and tan. The transition continues from spring to summer as flies and nymphs become increasingly lighter and larger. In autumn the cycle reverts back to darker and smaller flies and nymphs, until they are again very small and very dark during winter.

Spring fly-fishing in the Smokies lends itself to a wide array of techniques and tactics. Insofar as the trout and smallmouth bass actively feed now, it is tougher to do something that will not catch fish, than something that will catch them. This is probably overstating the wonders of spring a little, but it is such a wonderful time, particularly the last two weeks of May when caddis fly and mayfly hatches are rarely surpassed.

Admittedly, it is difficult to lump the fly-fishing conditions you will find in late March with those of late May. However, the transition is steady both in terms of the passage of the weeks, and the season's changes creeping toward the headwaters of these streams.

Summer Fly-fishing

Without question, summertime presents fly-fishermen in the Great Smoky Mountains National Park with more challenges than any other season. Rarely must anglers be more versatile than during the hot weather months of June, July, August, and early September. Anglers must be on guard against the muggy, often excessively humid heat, as well as tube riders seeking relief from the heat by riding the current. Throw in bloodthirsty mosquitoes and pesky "no-see-ums," and you see this is not a time to toss flies without possible consequences.

The park annually receives more rainfall than nearly any other region of the United States. A sizable portion of the annual rainfall comes in the form of summertime thunderstorms. It is not uncommon for the park to experience thunderstorms daily, or three times a day for week after week during the summer. Granted, a storm may pelt the Cosby area one day, then the next day it will shower at Raven Fork. Most thundershowers occur between mid-to late afternoon, but pre-dawn and early thunderstorms are certainly not uncommon.

Rather being a bane, rain is a blessing. Even the most harsh thunderstorms result in better angling than if the same stream is barely trickling along. This is not to say you should fly-fish when lightning bolts are lashing the sky—that would be insane. It also does not mean the initial high water provides prime fishing, although brown trout specialists such as Greg Ward live to dabble Muddler Minnows along undercut banks when thunderstorms turn otherwise gin-clear streams to the color of chocolate milk.

Rain accomplishes three very important things. It clouds the water, making it more difficult for trout to spot the approach of anglers. Increased flow levels enable trout and bass relegated to pools to move into feeding lanes. Runoff from the rain also washes a smorgasbord of terrestrial insects such as caterpillars, ants, jassids, beetles, grasshoppers, and inchworms into streams. The result is trout and bass feeding frenzies that usually last as long as the conditions that triggered this behavior continue.

It is rare for a fly-fisherman not to catch more and bigger trout and smallmouth bass following and sometimes during the rain. There is little question a majority of the bruiser brown trout caught in the Great Smoky Mountains National Park are landed under these conditions.

A word of warning regarding thunderstorms in these mountains. In recent years several people have been killed and injured by bolts of lightning. Whenever possible, seek safe refuge from lightning, and never fly-fish under these conditions. Also, it is not uncommon for thunderstorms to occur without your knowledge several miles upstream from where you are angling. As a result, the flow level of the stream may rise rapidly without warning. Classic flash floods are uncommon, but waters rising a foot or more rather quickly are not.

One afternoon I was fishing with my youngest son, Shae, who was then six (he has now made me a grandfather). We were in the lower reaches of the West Prong of the Little Pigeon River, upstream from the Sugarlands Ranger Headquarters, when the clear water suddenly turned brown. The sun was shining bright, but it had rained upstream from the Chimneys. We were on the side of the stream opposite the Transmountain Highway, where I had left my car. Putting Shae on my shoulders, I started crossing the stream at the tail of a pool that was thigh deep. Before I could get across the 50-foot-wide stream, the current rose above my waist. A minute after we got out, the stream rose another foot. Not before or since have I seen a stream in the Great Smoky Mountains National Park rise so rapidly with or without warning.

Unfortunately, not every fly-fishing trip to the streams coincides with rainy weather. Often we go fly-fishing on waters during the driest weather. This is undoubtedly the toughest of all times to cast for trout and bass on these waters. As a general rule, the farther upstream you fish, the more pronounced the effects of dry weather are on stream flow and on your odds for catching fish. Of course, it is possible to catch trout in slow, low, very clear water, especially if you fish very early in the morning or late in the evening. However, it requires highly accurate casting, faultless, drag-free presentation, and a lot of patience to catch even small trout from streams when those streams are running well below their normal flow rate.

Most hatches occur late in the evening or very early in the morning, which is when many trout do most of their feeding. Naturally, there are exceptions. I still do not understand why nice-size rainbow trout will rise to fly patterns during midday when these offerings are drifted over fast runs. I can understand why these fish prefer swift, well-oxygenated runs at this time when water temperatures are at their highest for the year and oxygen levels are their annual lowest. But what is mysterious is why they shun such offerings in the morning, only to seize them during the hottest part of the day.

In a nutshell, there is no such thing as a typical day of fly-fishing for trout during the summer at these waters. Virtually every type of response you can imagine can occur, and on consecutive days! It is like a drunken old angling buddy of mine once lamented, "Trout are like women, they choose the time and place to play." Such is summer fly-fishing in the streams of the Great Smoky Mountains National Park.

Autumn Fly-Fishing

One of my favorite seasons for fly-fishing in the Great Smoky Mountains National Park, autumn is a magical time. In many ways it is the very finest fly-fishing of the entire year. During autumn, these ancient rock piles take on a surrealistic feeling. Ablaze with spectacular oranges, scarlets, golds, and maroons, these mountains are back-dropped by cloudless, azure skies.

It is the only time of the year you can plan a trip to these streams with reasonable confidence that the weather reports from the previous day will deliver what was promised. It is time when the mornings are crisp enough to make a sweater feel good, and the afternoons are for fly-fishing in short sleeves. Bluebird skies beckon for day-long fishing trips, something many sane anglers here have forgone since early June.

Even though flow levels are rarely high, the trout are unusually cooperative. Fishery biologists say their high rate of feeding is instinctive, an effort to store fat for the oncoming winter. I contend the reason is the bright autumn foliage, which transforms the world above them from greens and blues to every color in the

Far and fine is often the rule during autumn.

rainbow. In my opinion, the stunning smattering of color throws the world of the trout out of kilter, causing them to feed with abandonment not seen by fly-fishermen in the Great Smoky Mountains since the caddis fly hatches of late May.

Autumn may be the driest time in the national park, but it does rain during this time. The best single day of fly-fishing I ever enjoyed on these waters occurred here on October 12, 1983, a day marked by a steady drizzle. Vic Stewart and I were fishing the West Prong of the Little Pigeon River only a mile upstream from the Sugarlands. It was cool, but when actively fishing wearing a raincoat, it was very comfortable.

The stream remained clear all day, and because it was quite low prior to the rain, it never rose high enough to create difficult wading or tough fishing at the fast runs typically resulting from heavy rainfall in the Smokies. We started out using No. 8 Joe's Hoppers, which could have been our luckiest move of the day. I do not believe anything we might have tossed could have matched the incredible results these simple fly patterns fetched.

Starting at eight o'clock in the morning, we fished our way upstream. Within an hour, we had caught and released more than a dozen rainbow trout more than 12 inches. These fish appeared to be ready to spawn. Females were full of eggs, and males were squirting milt. Their flanks were deep maroon, something I have only seen in these fish at this time of year (although rainbow trout also spawn in the spring and winter in the park).

It is not only the rainbow trout that behave differently at this time. Brown trout, which are noted for their nocturnal behavior, are now commonly encountered feeding with gusto at midstream, or even lying in the tails of streams in water so shallow their backs protrude from the surface. On many occasions I have nearly stepped on these fish, causing both of us quite a lot of excitement when our mutual discoveries were made.

Terrestrial fly patterns are often the rule for the day, but fly hatches also occur with remarkable predictability. Orange spinners work well late in the evening, as do a few Dun Variants. Early morning fly-fishing fun is often supplemented by hatches of the large pale caddis and little yellow stoneflies. Even when these are hatching at rates sufficient to attract trout, when stream flow levels are at seasonal lows, anglers must be astute at "far and fine" casting and presentation techniques.

Chapter 7

Stream Insects and Feathery Deceivers

Aquatic insects in the streams of the Smokies play an essential role in the diet of the trout. Fly-fishermen have long understood this relationship, fashioning their style of angling around this knowledge.

In many parts of the angling world, timetables giving the site and approximate time of the emergence of a well-known mayfly have been available for a number of years. The streams of the Smokies, however, are not dominated by any particular insect species or order, much the same as the mountainside flora is not dominated by any particular plant.

Aquatic insect populations are low in most cases. These streams are poor producers of food, primarily due to their acidic composition. Acid water is low in nutrients that are necessary for large concentrations of insects to exist. Other problems local insects must endure are acid rain and flash floods that scour the bottom of fragile life forms.

Just about every type of mayfly that occurs in the Appalachians is found in the park. However, the population densities of the aquatic insects are low, usually so low that even during peak emergence, they can sometimes play only a minor part in the trout's feeding habits.

Work done in researching the caddis flies of the Smokies by several noted zoologists reveals that the Tennessee Valley has one of the world's richest populations of caddis flies in the world. There are more than fifty genera of caddis flies found in the Smokies, according to Dr. David Etnier, professor of zoology at the University of Tennessee.

Stoneflies also do well in the swift, pollution-free waters of the park. The oxygen-rich, cascading streams harbor stonefly nymphs, important to the trout's diet during certain times of the year. These meaty morsels are eagerly seized by big brown trout.

Choosing the correct fly pattern is half the fun.

Watch the surface of the water carefully if you plan to attempt to match the hatch. Hatches of mayflies can be found on almost any day from January through October. During the cold months, hatches usually occur during the warmest hours of the afternoon. Later, during mid-spring, emergences can occur during mid-morning through late afternoon. By late spring, hatches will be encountered in early morning and then in late afternoon. Summer

Smallies are suckers for big hair flies.

is a time of limited, often sporadic insect activity, which usually occurs only during the early morning and around dusk. Matching the hatch is sometimes effective; however, presentation to these opportunistic feeders is really the key.

Traditional flies such as the Royal Coachman, Adams, Ginger Quill, and the Black Gnat find their way into the fly boxes of local anglers. Probably the most famous fly to come out of the Smokies was the Yallarhammar. There are numerous variations of this fly today on both sides of the mountains. It is basically a peacock herl-bodied wet fly, hackled with a split section of wing feather from a yellow-shafted woodpecker, known locally as a Yallarhammar. It is illegal to kill this bird or to sell flies using its plumage. (Yallarhammar flies are now being made with feathers from other species, dyed the correct shade of yellow.) However, the use of this fly is incredibly widespread, although its effectiveness is, in my opinion, no better than that of several other flies I could name. Other regional favorites include the Ramsey (it closely resembles a standard brown hackle), My Pet, Forky Tail Nymph, the nationally-known Tellico Nymph, the Grey Hackle Yellow, Cotton Top, and the Thunderhead. The Thunderhead is a Wulff-style dry hairwing fly.

Well-known flies such as the Adams, Coachman, Henryville Special, and several other established patterns are also used with great success inside the park. A dry fly that closely resembles a hairwing Adams, the Thunderhead, is the creation of Joe Hall of Bryson City. Hall is one of the greatest Smoky Mountains fly-tiers, and his clients have included such well-known anglers as Joe Brooks. Frank Young, another Carolina fly-tier, added one of the most interesting modifications to this fly I have ever seen. Young substituted the soft belly fur of a opossum in place of the kip tail usually used in making the Thunderhead. The result is equally interesting, as the fluffy 'possum fibers give the fly an added touch of drift as they fall gently on the surface of the water. The addition of the opossum hair makes this an all-hillbilly candidate.

When my original Smoky Mountain trout fishing guide was written in the late 1970s, every effort was made over a two-year research period to locate and interview the "great sages of the long rod" of the region. In my defense, I think I did a fairly good job, but made one glaring error in overlooking one of the true greats, Eddie George of Louisville, Tennessee, whom I interviewed in 1987. The creator of the famous George Nymph (which I mistakenly identified as the Cotton Top), George told me that he grew up fishing these streams prior to the Second World War with the old men of that era. A mayfly-style nymph of his creation, the George Nymph is nationally known as an effective trout taker, and cannot be topped as a year-round offering in the streams of the Great Smoky Mountains National Park.

My Pet, the Ugly Devil, the Quill Tail, and the Near Nuff all originated in western Carolina. The Grey Hackle Yellow, a delicate dry fly, is said to be the top choice of a number of Cherokee anglers. The Streaker Nymph is another fly of Carolina origin. It is very similar to the Tellico nymph, but is more slender and lighter in color. A favorite of many Hazel Creek regulars, it is tied to mock the abundant stickbait found in the flow of the park's creeks.

Unfortunately, space in this volume does not permit me to tell of every noted Smoky Mountain fly-fishing and fly-tying sage. The list would be long, and would certainly include such modern marvels as Marty Maxewell of Robbinsville, North Carolina, and Gary Cown of Knoxville, Tennessee, plus old-timers such as Levi Miller, Claude Gossett, Cap Weese, and Alvin Hayes, to name a few of the many fly-fishermen who have contributed the rich fly-fishing tradition of the Great Smoky Mountains.

Southern trout flies are beginning to become known nationally, as visiting anglers take these patterns home. Traditional patterns will take fish equally well. I know one top-flight dry fly-fisherman who uses a No.14 Royal Coachman exclusively.

When concentrating exclusively on smallmouth and rock bass fly suggestions, always include the Muddler Minnow (sizes No.6 and No.8), hellgrammite imitations (sizes No.6 to No.4), Olive Wooly Boogers (sizes No.6 to No. 8), and the Green Inch (sizes No.4 to No.8). Dace-style streamers (sizes No.4 to No.8) and crayfish imitators (sizes No.2 to No.6) are also highly effective on these waters.

The following is an aquatic insect emergence table put in this book to cover the tastes and needs of the most discriminating fly-fishermen. It is merely a general guideline that may or may not apply precisely to the time and place you may be fishing in the Smokies. Some streams have superior benthic communities of macroinvertebrates, and hatches may be off as much as two weeks or more due to weather and other considerations.

Hatches and Matches for Aquatic Insects

Late Winter Hatches and Matches for Aquatic Insects

Common name	Days	Time	Matching dry pattern
Blue Dun	Late January thru February	Mid-day	Male Adams (No.14-No.16)
Dun Caddis	January and February	Late morning/ afternoon	Elk Wing Caddis (No.16) Bucktail Caddis (No. 14 to No.16) Dark Blue Dun (No.16 to No.18) Adam Caddis (No.14)

Blue Quill	Mid-to late February	Late morning/ mid-afternoon	Adams Variant (No.16) Thunderhead (No.16) Blue Quill (No.16) Dark Brown Spinner (No.16)
Blue-Winged Olive (or Baetis)	Late January to mid-February	Mid-day	Royal Wulff (No.14 to No.18) Adams Parachute (No.16 to No.18)
Winter Black Stonefly	January thru February	All day	(See nymphs)
Winter Brown (or Dark Stonefly)	Mid-to late February	Mid-day	Deer Hair (No.12 to No.16) Pickett Fence (No.14 to No.16) Little Brown Stone (No.14) Dark Elkwing Caddis (No.14)
Olive Midge	January thru February	Mid-day	Adams Variant (No.18 to No.20) Gnats (No.18 to No.22)

Early Spring Hatches and Matches for Aquatic Insects

Common name	Days	Time	Matching dry pattern
Blue Dun	March and thru April	Mid-day	Male Adams (No.12 to No.14) Grey Hackle (No.12 to No.14) Thunderhead (No.12)
Dun Caddis	March and April	Most of the day	Elk Wing Caddis (No.16) Bucktail Caddis (No.14 to No.16) Dark Blue Dun (No.16 to No.18) Adam Caddis (No.14)
Blue Quill	March and April	Mid-day	Adams (No.16) Thunderhead (No.16) Blue Quill (No.16) Dark Brown Spinner (No.16)
Blue-Winged Olive (or Baetis)	March and April	Mid-day	Pheasant Tail (No.18) Adams Parachute (No.16 to No.18)
Early Dark Stonefly	March and April	All day	Buck Tail Caddis (No.14 to No.16)
Brown (or Dark) Stonefly	Mid-to late March (later at higher elevations)	Mid-day	Deer Hair (No.12 to No.16) Pickett Fence (No.14 to No.16 Little Brown Stone (No.14)

Red Quill	Late March thru April	Early to late afternoon	Red Quill (No.12 (to No.16 Henderickson (No.12 to No.14)
Quill Gordon	Early March thru early April (later at higher elevations)	Mid-day	Male Adams (No.12 to No.16) Royal Wulff (No.14) Quill Gordon (No.14 to No.16)
March Brown	Mid-March thru April	Mid-day	March Brown (No.12 to No.16) Royal Wulff (No.12 to No.14)
Tawny (or Yellow) Stonefly	Late March thru April	Mid-day	Buck Tail Caddis (No.14 to No.16) Yellow Palmer (No.12 to No.14) Pickett Fence (No.14) Elk Wing Caddis (No.14 to No.16) Greenbriar Special (No.14)
Giant Stones (Black)	Late March thru April	Early morning	(See nymphs)
Gray Fox	Most of April	Mid-to late afternoon	Grey Fox (No.12 to late afternoon No.16)
Green Drake	Last week of April	Late morning and late afternoon	Green Drake (No.10 to No.12)
Gray/Brown Stonefly	Late April	Mid-day	Elk Wing Caddis (No.10 to No.14)

Apple Green Caddis	Late April	Mid-to late afternoon	Greenbriar Special (No.14 to No.18) Yellow Palmer (No.16 to No.18) green-tied Elk Wing Caddis (No.16 to No.18)
Light Cahill	Late April	Early morning and late afternoon	Light Cahill (No.12 to No.16)
Midges	March and April	Mid-day	Gnats (No.18 to No. 24) Light Cahill (No.22 to No.24)

Late Spring/Early Summer Hatches and Matches for Aquatic Insects

Common name	Days	Time	Matching dry pattern
Dun Caddis	May and April	Mid-day	Elk Wing Caddis (No.16) Bucktail Caddis (No.14 to No.16) Dark Blue Dun Royal Trude (No.14 to No.16)
March Brown	May (most common at higher elevations)	Mid-day	March Brown (No.12 to No.16) Royal Wulff (No.12 to No.14)
Giant Stones (Black)	May and June	Early morning	(See nymphs)
Grey Fox	May (and June at higher elevations)	Late afternoon	Grey Fox (No.12 to No.14)

Green Drake	May (and early June at higher elevations)	Late morning and late afternoon	Green Drake (No.10 to No.12)
Golden Stonefly	May (and June at higher elevations)	Mid-day	Yellow Palmer (No.14 to No.16) Chuck Caddis (No.14 to No.16)
Little Yellow Stonefly	May and June	Early morning, late evening	Yellow Palmer (No.14 to No.18)
Apple Green Caddis	May and June	Mid-day	Greenbriar Special (No.10 to No.14) Yellow Palmer (No.12 to No.14) green-tied Elk Wing Caddis (No.10 to No.12)
Little Green Caddis	May (and June at higher elevations)	Late afternoon	Greenbriar Special (No.14 to No.18) Pickett Fence (No.18)
Light Cahill	May and June	Early morning and late afternoon	Light Cahill (No.10 to No.14) Yellow Humpy (No.10 to No.12)
Sulphur Dun	May and June	Mid-day to late evening	Yellow Humpy (No.16 to No.18) Light Cahill (No.16 to No.1)
Pink Lady (or Orange Spinner)	May and June	Late afternoon to dark	Orange Spinner (No.12 to No.14) Orange Palmer (No.12 to No.14)

Black Caddis	May (and early June at higher elevations)	Mid-day to late evening	Dark Brown Elk Wing (No.14 to No.16)
Brown Stonefly	May and June	Very early morning	Pickett Fence (No.10 to No.12)
Midges	May and June	Mid-day	Gnats (No.18 No.24) Light Cahill (No.20 to No.24)

Late Summer Hatches and Matches for Aquatic Insects

Common name	Days	Time	Matching dry pattern
Black Quill	July (and early August at higher elevations)	Late evening	Grey Fox (No.14)
Giant Yellow	July (and early August at higher elevations)	Late evening	Thunderhead (No.10) Light Cahill (No.10 to No.12)
Dun Variant	July and August	Late evening	Dun Variant (No.10 and No.12)
Grey Brown Caddis	July and August	Late afternoon until dark	Dark Elk Wing (No.14 to No.18) Chuck Caddis (No.14 to No.18)
Golden Stonefly	July and August	Pre-dawn/ dusk	Yellow Palmer (No.14 to No.16) Greenbriar Special (No.14 to No.16)

Light (or Tan) Caddis	July and August	Late evening until dark	Greenbriar Caddis (No.14 to No.16) Tan Elk Wing Caddis (No.14 to No.18)
Little Yellow and Little Green Stoneflies	July and August	Early morning late evening	Yellow Palmer (No.14 to No.18) Green Palmer (No.14 to No.16)
Light Cahill	July and August	Late afternoon until dark	Light Cahill (No.12 to No.16) Yellow Humpy (No.14 to No.16)
Dark Bluewing Olive	July and August	Late afternoon until dark	Female Adams (No.14 to No.18)
Trico-Black and White	Late July thru August	Early morning to mid-morning	Trico Spinner (No.18 to No.22)
Pink Lady (or Orange Spinner)	July (and August at higher elevations)	Late afternoon to dark	Orange Spinner (No.12 to No.14) Orange Palmer (No.12 to No.14)
Brown Stonefly	July and August	Early morning and late evening	(See nymphs)
Cream Midges	July and August	Most of the day	Gnats (No.20 to No.24) Light Cahill (No.20 to No.24)

Early Autumn Hatches and Matches for Aquatic Insects

Common name	Days	Time	Matching dry pattern
Pink Lady (or Orange Spinner)	Early September	Late afternoon to dark	Orange Spinner (No.12 to No.14) Orange Palmer (No.12 to No.14)
Large Pale Caddis	September	Early morning late evening	Elk Wing Caddis (No.6 to No.10)
Dun Variant	September	Late evening	Dun Variant (No.10 to No.12) Adams (No.10 to No.12)
Golden Stonefly	September (and October at higher elevations)	Pre-dawn/dusk	(See nymphs)
Little Yellow and Little Green Stoneflies	September	Early morning late evening	Yellow Palmer (No.14 to No.18) Green Palmer (No.14 to No.16)
Dark Bluewing Olive	September and October	Early afternoon until dark	Female Adams (No.22 to No.24)
Trico-Black and White	Late September thru October	Early morning	Trico Spinner (No.18 to No.22)
Cream Midges	Late September thru October	Most of the day	Gnats (No.20 to No.24) Light Cahill No.20 to No.24)

Late Autumn/Early Winter Hatches and Matches for Aquatic Insects

Common name	Days	Time	Matching dry pattern
Blue Quill	November	Mid-day	Adams (No.16) Thunderhead (No.16) Blue Quill (No.16)
Blue-Winged Olive (or Baetis)	November	Mid-day	Thunderhead (No.16 to No.18) Adams (No.16 to No.18)
Large Pale Caddis	Early November	Early morning late evening	Elk Wing Caddis (No.6 to No.10)
Dun Caddis	November	Mid-day	Elk Wing Caddis (No.14 to No.18) Squash Bug (No.14)
Yellow Caddis	November	Early morning Mid-day	Yellow Palmer (No.14 to No.18) Blonde Elk Wing Caddis (No.14 to No.16) Royal Trude (No.14 to No.16)
Grey Midges	November	Mid-day	Gnats (No.20 to No.24) Adams (No.20 to No.24)

Late Winter Hatches and Matches for Nymphs for Aquatic Insects

Common name	Days	Time	Matching dry pattern
Blue Dun	Late January thru February	Mid-day	My Pet (No.14 to No.16)
Dun Caddis	January and February	Late morning/ afternoon	Yallarhammar (No.16) Solomon's Black Pupa (No.14 to No.16)
Blue Quill	Mid-to late February	Late morning/ mid-afternoon	Zug Bug (No.16) George's Nymph (No.12)
Blue Winged-Olive (or Baetis)	Late January to mid-February	Mid-day	Pheasant Tail (No.18) My Pet (No.16 to No.18)
Winter Black Stonefly	January thru February	All day	Montana Stonefly (No.12 to No.16) George's Nymph (No.14 to No.16)
Winter Brown (or Dark Stonefly)	Mid-to late February	Mid-day	Brown Stonefly (No.10 to No.14)
Olive Midge	January thru February	Mid-day	My Pet (No.18 to No.20)

Spring Hatches and Matches for Nymphs for Aquatic Insects

Common name	Days	Time	Matching dry pattern
Blue Dun	March thru February	Mid-day	My Pet (No.12 to No.14) Pheasant Tail (No.12 to No.14)
Dun Caddis	March and April	Most of the day	Stickbait (No.12) Hare's Ear (No.14 to No.16)
Blue Quill	March and April	Mid-day	Blue Quill Nymph (No.16) Muskrat (No.14 to No.16)
Blue-Winged Olive (or Baetis)	March and April	Mid-day	Pheasant Tail (No.18) Hare's Ear (No.16 to No.18)
Early Dark Stonefly	March and April	All day	Forky Tail Nymph (No.12 to No.14)
Brown (or Dark Stonefly)	Mid-to late March	Mid-day	Forky Tail Nymph (No.12 to No.14) Brown Stone No.10)
Red Quill	Late March thru April	Early to late afternoon	Hendrickson Nymph (No.12 to No.14) Muskrat (No.12 to No.14)
Quill Gordon	Early March thru early April	Mid-day	Hare's Ear (No.12 to No.14) Quill Gordon Nymph (No.14 to No.16)

March Brown	Mid-March thru April	Mid-day	March Brown Nymph (No.12 to No.16) Hare's Ear (No.12 to No.14)
Tawny (or Yellow) Stonefly	Late March thru April	Mid-day	Yallarhammar (No.10 to No.14) Forky Tail (No.12 to No.14) Yellow Stonefly Nymph (No.10 to No.12)
Giant Stones (Black)	Late March thru April	Early morning	Montana Nymph (No.4 to No.10) Black Stonefly Nymph (No.4 to No.6) Crow Fly (No.4 to No.8) Dark Stone (No.10)
Grey Fox	Most of April	Mid- to late afternoon	Muskrat (No.12 to No.14) Hare's Ear (No.10 to No.12) My Pet (No.10)
Green Drake	Last week of April	Late morning and late afternoon	Green Nymph (No.10 to No.12) My Pet (No.10 to No.8)
Grey/Brown Stonefly	Late April	Mid-day	Dark Stone (No.10 to No.12) Olive Stone (No.10 to No.12)
Apple Green Caddis	Late April	Mid- to late afternoon	Green-tied Tellico Nymph (No.14 to No.18) Zug Bug (No.16)

| Light Cahill | Late April | Early morning and late afternoon | Light Cahill Nymph (No.12 to No.14) Cotton Top (No.12) George Nymph (No.12 to No.14) |
| Midges | March and April | Mid-day | George Nymph (No.18 to No.22) |

Hatches and Matches for Nymphs

Late Spring/Early Summer Hatches and Matches for Nymphs

Common name	Days	Time	Matching dry pattern
Dun Caddis	May and April	Mid-day	Stickbait (No.12) Hare's Ear (No.14 to No.16)
March Brown	May (most common at higher elevations)	Mid-day	March Brown Nymph (No.12 to No.14) Hare's Ear (No.12 to No.14)
Giant Stones (Black)	May and June	Early morning	Montana Nymph (No.4 to No.10) Black Stonefly Nymph (No.4 to No.6) Crow Fly (No.4 to No.8) Dark Stone (No.10)
Grey Fox	May (and June at higher elevations)	Late afternoon	Muskrat (No.12 to No.14) Hare's Ear (No.10 to No.12) My Pet (No.10)

Green Drake	May	Late morning and late afternoon	Green Nymph (No.10 to No.12) My Pet (No.10 to No.8)
Golden Stonefly	May	Mid-day	Golden Stonefly Nymph (No.12 to No.16) Yellow Stone (No.10 to No.14)
Little Yellow Stonefly	May and June	Early morning late evening	Yellow Stone (No.12 to No.14)
Apple Green Caddis	May and June	Mid-day thru afternoon	Green-tied Tellico Nymph (No.14 to No.18) Zug Bug (No.16)
Little Green Caddis	May	Late afternoon	Tellico Nymph (No.14 to No.16) Yallarhammar (No.14)
Light Cahill	May and June	Early morning and late afternoon	Light Cahill Nymph (No.10 to No.12)
Sulphur Dun	May and June	Mid-day to late evening	Sulphur Emerger (No.14 to No.16) Yallarhammar (No.12 to No.14)
Pink Lady (or Orange Spinner)	May and June	Late afternoon to dark	Pink Lady (No.10 to No.12) orange-tied Tellico Nymph (No.10 to No.12)

Black Caddis	May (and June at higher elevations)	Mid-day to late evening	Dark Brown Pupa (No.14 to No.16) My Pet (No.16)
Brown Stonefly	May and June	Very early morning	Brown Stone (No.10 to No.12) Forky Tail (No.10 to No.12)
Midges	May and June	Mid-day	George Nymph (No.18 to No.24)

Late Summer Hatches and Matches for Nymphs

Common name	Days	Time	Matching dry pattern
Black Quill	July	Late evening	George Nymph (No.12 to No.14)
Giant Yellow	July	Late evening	Mayfly Nymph (No.10) Light Cahill Nymph (No.10 to No.12)
Dun Variant	July and August	Late evening	Wooly Booger (No.10 and No.12) Yallarhammar (No.10 to No.14)
Grey Brown Caddis	July and August	Late afternoon until dark	Tellico Nymph (No.14 to No.16) Cotton Top (No.12 to No.16)
Golden Stonefly	July and August	Pre-dawn/ dusk	Yellow Stone (No.12 to No.14)

Light (or Tan)	July and August	Late evening until dark	Stickbait (No.12 to No.14) Tan Caddis Solomon (No.14 to No.16) Tellico Nymph (No.12 to No.16)
Little Yellow	July and August	Early morning late evening	Yellow Stone (No.14 to No.16)
Little Green Stoneflies	July and August	Early morning late evening	Green Pupa (No.14 to No.16)
Light Cahill	July and August	Late afternoon until dark	Light Cahill Nymph (No.12 to No.16) Yellow Mayfly (No.14 to No.16)
Dark Bluewing Olive	July and August	Late afternoon until dark	Yallarhammar (No.14 to No.18) Bluewing Olive Nymph (No.14 to No.18)
Trico-Black and White	Late July thru August	Early morning to mid-morning	George Nymph (No.18 to No.22)
Pink Lady (or Orange Spinner)	July (and early August at higher elevations)	Late afternoon	Pink Lady (No.12 to No.14) Yallarhammar (No.12 to No.14)
Brown Stonefly	July and August	Early morning and late evening	Forky Tail (No.8 to No.12) Brown Stone (No.8 to No.10)
Cream Midges	July and August	Most of the day	Cotton Top (No.20 to No.24)

Early Autumn Hatches and Matches for Nymphs

Common name	Days	Time	Matching dry pattern
Pink Lady (or Orange Spinner)	Early September (late September at higher elevations)	Late afternoon to dark	Pink Lady (No.12 to No.14)
Large Pale Caddis	September	Early morning Late evening	Solomon Pupa (No.6 to No.10) Yallarhammar (No.10)
Dun Variant	September	Late evening	Tellico Nymph (No.10 and No.12)
Golden Stonefly	September	Pre-dawn/dusk	Golden Stone Nymph (No.4 to No.10)
Little Yellow and Little Green Stoneflies	September	Early morning late evening	Yellow Stone (No.14 to No.18) Green Pupa (No.14 to No.16)
Dark Bluewing Olive	September (and thru mid-October at higher elevations)	Early afternoon until dark	Bluewing Olive Nymph (No.22 to No.24)
Trico-Black and White	Late July thru August	Early morning	George Nymph (No.18 to No.22)
Cream Midges	July and August	Most of the day	Cotton Top (No.20 to No.24)

Late Autumn/Early Winter Hatches and Matches for Nymphs

Common name	Days	Time	Matching dry pattern
Blue Quill	November	Mid-day	Blue Quill Nymph (No.16) Muskrat (No.14 to No.16)
Blue-Winged Olive (or Baetis)	November	Mid-day	Pheasant Tail (No.18) Hare's Ear (No.16 to No.18)
Large Pale Caddis	Early November	Early morning late evening	Solomon Pupa Caddis (No.6 to No.10) Yallarhammar (No.10)
Dun Caddis	November	Mid-day	Caddis Pupa (No.14 to No.18) (No.12)
Yellow Caddis	November	Early morning mid-day	Yallarhammar (No.14 to No.18) Tellico Nymph (No.14 to No.16)
Grey Midges	November	Mid-day	George Nymph (No.20)

Non-Aquatic Insect Fly Pattern/Time Recommendations

The following terrestrial patterns are recommended for use on all streams in the Great Smoky Mountains National Park from mid-June through late October: Little River Ant (sizes No.10 to No.18), Joe's Hopper (sizes No.4 to No.10), and Japanese Beetle (No.12).

The following streamer patterns are recommended for use on all streams in the Great Smoky Mountains National Park year-round: Black Nose Dace (sizes No.6 to No.12), Muddler Minnow (sizes No.4 to No.8), Olive Wooly Booger (sizes No.6 to No.8), Grey Ghost (sizes No.6 to No.10), Little Rainbow Trout (sizes No.8 to No.10), and Spuddler (sizes No.6 to No.8).

There are several old patterns that are well-known to many local fly-fishermen, most notably the Tellico Nymph and the notorious Yallarhammar. (A word of caution: only carry Yallarhammar flies made with feathers dyed to match the amber-hued wing feathers of the yellow-shafted flicker, or yellowhammer woodpecker. Rangers who catch anglers using flies with real yellowhammer feathers are not happy people.)

Other local patterns noted earlier in the fly emergence/fly pattern chart, as well as those noted in my first book, include the Stickbait, Streaker Nymph, George Nymph, My Pet, Forky Tail, Cotton Top, Squash Bug, Thunderhead, Ellison's Greenbriar Special, Ugly Devil, Ramsey Brown Hackle, Little River Ant, Copperhead, Jim Charley, Wood Bee, Tennessee Wulff, Secret Weapon, Red Fox Squirrel Nymph, Smoky Mountain Caddis, Yellow Palmer, and Grey Hackle Yellow. These are only a few of the many patterns old and modern fly-tiers have created in this region. Each of the patterns and the men who created them could be made into additional chapters in this fly-fishing guide book to the greatest angling destination in the eastern United States.

I, and a large number of other Smoky Mountains fly-fishermen, find the above tables to be somewhat cumbersome, which is largely why I chose not to include such a list in my previous fishing guidebooks to park waters. (It was at the request of many other anglers that it is now offered.) My theory on fishing is to keep it as simple as possible. My friend Greg Ward, owner of Rocky Top Outfitters located in Pigeon Forge, Tennessee, who is also a master fly-fisherman, has developed what I believe is the best, most down-to-earth approach to understanding aquatic fly hatches in the streams of the Great Smoky Mountains National Park.

Like me, he doesn't give a hoot in Hell about most of the information that can be garnered by studying fly identification or hatch charts. He carries no more than a dozen different flies in his fly boxes. Chapter 8 contains Ward's advice.

Chapter 8

Common Sense Approach to Smoky Mountain Fly-Fishing

by Greg Ward

For almost two decades, I have spent an embarrassing portion of my life waist-deep in the streams of the Great Smoky Mountains National Park. Much of that time I have also earned all or a portion of my income as a licensed fishing guide in the national park. I fish dry flies almost exclusively for two reasons: nothing in the world thrills me more than seeing a trout take a fly from the surface, and it allows me totally escape the modern world. The fact that you catch bigger trout on dry flies only makes it even better. During this time I have developed what I refer to as my "Ten Dry Fly Theory."

First, allow me to tell you what I do not pay attention to, starting with the midges. Sure, trout eat them, and some fly-fishermen catch fish on midge patterns, but forget them—they are not worthy of further discussion. I also do not pay attention to the stoneflies. Yes, they are big, and yes, trout do feed on them; however, for dry fly-fishing they are not worth singling out, as for the most part caddis fly imitators effectively match emerging stoneflies. In my opinion, any caddis fly or mayfly dry fly pattern can effectively imitate a stonefly of its size and color. A trout cannot see the top of a dry fly, which is the only real difference in the appearance of a caddis fly, mayfly, or stonefly dry fly pattern.

Next, I do not fly-fish the waters of the Smokies from around the first of November through mid-December. That is when these streams are largely clogged with leaves from the hardwoods, which result in large amounts of tannic acid in the water. However, from mid-December through February I highly recommend angling with dry flies in the park, but only when the air temperature is at least forty-seven degrees Fahrenheit. That is the magic time for fly activity. The warmer its gets, and the more sunshine and less wind you have, the better things are on these waters.

Winter fly hatches present you with the challenge of matching may and caddis flies that are generally small (sizes No.14 to No.16) and predominantly black to dark brown in color. A dry fly you should always carry at this time is the Bluewing Olive (sizes No.14 to No.16). If you must nymph fish, nothing tops a Pheasant Tail (sizes No.14 to No.16), and Caddis Pupa (sizes No. 14 to No.16) and if you aren't going to dry fly-fish, why not go whole hog and drag a streamer? My favorite streamer pattern at this time is a Muddler Minnow (size No.6 to No.8) trimmed with a white turkey feather, and an Olive Wooly Booger (size No.6). The addition of the white turkey feather to the Muddler Minnow is the real key.

In March, the streams of the Great Smoky Mountains National Park undergo a predictable transition, and the flies become a little larger and less dark in color. Again, never go fishing without a few Bluewing Olives (size No.14), as well as the Thunderhead (sizes No.14 to No.16), or my current personal favorite, the Little Black Caddis (sizes No.14 to No.16), which matches the typically large hatches of these prolific aquatic insects. If you must drift nymphs during March, you can do no better than to tie on a Cream Caddis Pupa (size No.14). The only exception to this is when fly-fishing the Little River, where the Olive Caddis Pupa (size No.14) is a better choice.

The arrival of April is a continuation of the seasonal coloration transition from inky and black in winter, to lighter (or more neutral) colors in spring, and even lighter colors during the summer months. My favorite mayfly imitator is the Male Adams (sizes No.10 to No.14). The nymph of the month is the Hare's Ear (sizes No.12 to No.14).

May and June rank among the top, if not the best, dry fly-fishing months of the year. My favorite dry fly during May is the Male Adams (sizes No.10 to No.14), followed by the Light Cahill (sizes No.10 to No.14). I commonly use size No.10 Adams, and even size No.8 Adams, which are my secret weapons at this time for catching trophy-class brown trout. To match the bright green caddis flies common to this month, cast the Fluorescent Green

Tennessee Wulff (sizes No.12 to No.14) or a Fluorescent Green Humpy (sizes No.12 to No.14).

July and August are also prime months for dry fly-fishing. Again, the Fluorescent Green Tennessee Wulff (sizes No.12 to No.14) and a Fluorescent Green Humpy (sizes No.12 to No.14) are good choices. However, my favorites remain the Adams(sizes No.10 to No.12), and the Thunderhead (sizes No.10 to No.12). This is also when I switch to terrestrial insect patterns such as ants and grasshoppers. I like big 'hoppers (sizes No.8 to No.4). This is also a great time to nymph fish using a Fluorescent Green Inch Worm (sizes No.12 to No.14).

Early autumn dry fly-fishing is excellent in the Great Smoky Mountains National Park. My favorite then, as it was in the preceding months, is the Adams (sizes No.10 to No.12), followed by the Orange Palmer (sizes No.10 to No.12), which matches the fall hatch of orangish-colored caddis flies in the park. Nymph fishermen will discover they do better switching to smaller and darker nymph patterns, as the dark-to-light-to-dark cycle is now making its full circle beneath the surface of these streams.

The aquatic insects of the Great Smoky Mountains National Park are incredibly simple to understand. The key to catching trout here is to remember these insects are small and dark during the winter months. As spring arrives, they become slightly larger and lighter in color. During the summer months, stream insects are their largest and lightest in color. This is also when these fish have their greatest access to terrestrial insects, such as jassids, beetles, bees, ants, and grasshoppers. The latter is by far the most important to those wishing to catch large trout. It is a simple approach that works very well.

My gear recommendations are also simple. Flyrods between 7.5 and 9.5 feet are recommended. A few people push 6- to 7-foot rods for use on small streams, but such short rods do not permit you to mend line drag as effectively as longer rods. I also advise anglers guided by my staff to wear camouflage clothing and wading boots with felt soles. Camo helps you blend in with your surroundings, while the felt soles enable you to wade the waters with significantly fewer slips and tumbles.

In conclusion, if I were limited to a single dry fly, it would be a size No.12 Male Adams. I can catch trout year round on this particularly deadly pattern. There is always some meaty, tasty looking neutral-colored mayfly hatching on these streams, and the trout love them. If I only had one nymph, it would be a properly presented No.14 Gold Ear's Hare. Proper presentation is the secret to catching trout in the Great Smoky Mountains National Park, or anywhere else.

If you have any questions about fly-fishing in and around the Great Smoky Mountains National Park, please do not hesitate to contact me at Rocky Top Outfitters; 2721 Parkway; Pigeon Forge, Tennessee 37863; 423-429-3474.

Chapter 9

Ben Craig: Master Fly-Tyer of the Smokies

The region collectively known as the Great Smoky Mountain National Park has produced many of Dixie's best-known tyers of feathery trout flies. Nationally-known patterns such as the Yallarhammer and Tellico Nymph have origins richly steeped in the fly-tying lore of these misty mountains. In fact, over the course of the last three decades, I have spoken with at least three fly-tyers (all now dead) who told me they recall seeing the now-famous Wulff-style hair wing tied dry flies long before Lee Wulff is reported to have initiated this wise practice.

Life has been good, allowing me to meet such fly-tying legends as Kirk Jenkins, Earnest Ramsey, Joe Hall, Eddie George, and dozens and dozens of other local fly-tyers. While each of these fly-tyers has earned his own degree of greatness, none has reached the pinnacle of this craft like Ben Craig of Waynesville, North Carolina. At least a second-generation tyer, this sixty-five-year-old trout fishing expert and master fly-tyer not only originated many of the fly patterns we use today, but also trained or influenced virtually everyone now tying flies in western North Carolina.

"I've been tying flies for over half a century," notes Craig, as we chatted in his fly-tying parlor. Adorned with enough feathers, fur, thread, and yard to keep a dozen fly-tyers in business for years, the room also houses a portion of his collection of vintage bamboo flyrods. A prize possession, a mount of a native 13-inch speckled trout, hung beside the slightly-built Craig as we conversed. His fly-tying parlor features wildlife art and every imaginable sort of feather and fur.

One entire wall of shelves in Craig's fly-tying parlor stores his current inventory of flies, which is never very high, as a result of the high demand for his tying efforts. Craig sells his flies to anglers all across the country, including to such notable sports-men as Dick Kirby, owner of Quaker Boy Game Calls of Pennsylvania.

"As a youngster, I learned to tie flies by watching my father, who was a lifelong trout fisherman fond of fly-fishing. He kept his fly-tying material in a cardboard box, buying only thread and hooks for creating his flies. I don't think there are many farms in a three-county area where he and I didn't chase down roosters to pick a few choice hackles from their necks.

"As a young fly-tyer, my friends and I were exceptionally fond of floating Royal Coachman dries at the streams of the Great Smoky Mountains National Park. The most deadly addition we discovered for our home-tied Royal Coachman flies was the bright red plastic band used to seal packs of Lucky Strike cigarettes. Early on Saturday mornings, we would go to downtown Waynesville to patrol the streets for discarded plastic bands for making these flies."

Ben Craig shares much of the same fly-fishing and fly selection philosophy of this writer and many others in and around the Great Smoky Mountains National Park. Proper presentation of your fly and a general understanding of the region's aquatic insect com-munity are far more important than knowing the Latin name for three dozen different species of mayfly. Craig's all-time favorite fly pattern is Adams. Of course, he carries these in a wide assortment of sizes and varieties, including the Adams Parachute and Adams Wulff, as well as the Black Adams and the Adams Variant. In addi-tion to this, Craig also varies the body of the Adams he fishes, using dark bodies in late winter and spring, and lighter bodies in summer. Similarly, he switches from a dark brown hackle in win-ter and spring, to a grizzly hackle in summer.

Craig is a treasure-trove of knowledge on fly-fishing for trout in the Great Smoky Mountains National Park. While he prefers to keep his fly pattern selection ultra simple, he has several recom-mendations he knows will consistently produce trout in these waters at certain times of the year. One favorite is the well-known Thunderhead and the Chocolate Thunderhead, which in his opin-ion differ little from an Adams Wulff. He believes the Chocolate Thunderhead is particularly effective during May and June.

Another fly pattern recommended by Craig is the Elk Wing Hopper, a high-riding imitation of the grasshoppers that are com-mon to the region and relished by trout and bass in these streams.

The secret to making a highly deadly Elk Wing Hopper is dressing its flanks with a speckled feather from a bronze-colored domestic turkey. Extremely rare, such matched speckled feathers are Craig's most prized fly-tying material.

The Orange Palmer is another fly pattern Craig recommends anglers carry when visiting the streams of the Great Smoky Mountains National Park. A highly efficient imitation of the orange-colored caddis flies common to these waters, the Orange Palmer is a simplistic pattern Craig says came about around twenty-five years ago. He is not certain, but strongly believes the Orange Palmer pattern originated in the hollows of Haywood County, North Carolina.

Craig also likes the Tellico Nymph for mimicking emerging caddis pupa, but believes nothing tops the old-fashioned Stickbait Nymph for this chore. He ties his from a special latex material he has located that perfectly matches the dingy, yellowish-white color of these highly-sought-after trout foods. Being a long-time angler here, Craig is quick to point out that nothing ever whipped onto a hook by a fly-tyer as well as the real thing—soft, pulpy stickbait.

The Green Inchworm is another pattern highly recommended by Craig. This, along with a Sourwood Worm fly he created at the request of his son, Kevin, is deadly for taking trout during the late spring and summer months.

When asked about the older patterns used over the years in the Great Smoky Mountains National Park, Craig notes that while the Yallarhammar may be one of, if not the, oldest patterns here, its trout-catching magic is over-rated.

A lot of the local fly-fishermen swear by the Yallarhammar, but I can name a dozen fly patterns that will out-produce this old-timey pattern. In fact, the best way to catch trout on a Yallarhammar is to put stickbait on it!

"Indeed, I have tied many of them, having split as many yellow flicker wings as anyone, I suppose. And because there is still considerable demand for Yallarhammar flies, I still tie them, but not with the traditional yellow flicker feathers. I have developed a dyed substitute that is just as effective as the real thing, and certainly less likely to get you in trouble with park rangers, who are always alert for Yallarhammar flies made from the feathers of the protected birds they are named for," says Craig.

Craig ties what he calls the traditional Yallarhammar fly, which is a full-length Palmer hackle. He says this is the original way the fly was tied, not the shortcut version found in Tennessee. The Tennessee Yallarhammar usually has a peacock herl body, and two to three wraps of yellow flicker feather dressing, although I have used many of the Palmer hackled version referred to by Craig, tied by Earnest Ramsey of Muddy Creek, Tennessee.

"Another old fly rarely seen these days is the Wasp Nymph, which I believe was a caddis fly imitator. The Webber Forked Tail (which may have been tied by Kirk Jenkins of Newport, Tennessee, for the Webber Company) was another favorite pattern, as was the Pale Watery Dun. The latter fly has large mallard wings, and a large forked tail that enables it to ride high in the water."

Ben Craig is the quintessential Smoky Mountains fly-tyer. An ordained deacon in his Southern Baptist Church, he probably spends less money to produce more flies than anyone else. Tucked away in his fly-tying parlor are remnants of the rabbit fur coats popular among women a few years ago. Rather than buy expensive fur dubbing, Craig places chunks from these coats and other sources in a blender. In three seconds, he has a handful of fur dubbing equal to that sold in fly shops. Craig receives all types of fur and feathers, from caribou and elk, to wild turkey and wood duck, from his many hunting friends.

Craig has been asked to help write books on fly-tying in the Great Smoky Mountains, as well as to help produce instructional videos on how to tie the many flies of the region. However, to date, this is the first time he has ever allowed a writer to publish this information.

"Trout fishing in the Great Smoky Mountains National Park is a very personal thing for me. In recent years it has become increasingly difficult to find a stretch of stream where tubers and tourists don't pester you to death," said Craig. "I have shared my tying knowledge with many local tyers, but my privacy is extremely important to me."

Chapter 10

Kirk's Sixteen Favorite Fly Patterns

Everyone who has fly-fished the streams of the Great Smoky Mountains National Park for as long as I have develops a group of favorite fly patterns they prefer not to go astream without. The following are my sixteen favorite flies, which rarely let me down.

Adams Dry

A pattern created shortly after the First World War by fly-tyer Len Holliday, the Adams Dry is a remarkably versatile and durable trout fly. Extremely deadly in the Smokies and nearly everywhere else, the Adams is constructed of naturally buoyant muskrat fur, which can modified to make the fly light in coloration or inky dark. I carry these flies in sizes No.10 to No.18. An excellent choice for searching out trout almost twelve months of the year, this so-called searcher pattern also effectively matches several adult and emerging mayfly species common to the Great Smoky Mountains National Park.

Light Cahill Dry

Reportedly of Scottish origins, the Cahill is a long-time favorite on park waters. Most effective between late spring and early autumn, this mayfly imitator is my favorite "evening hatch" offering. In his *Art Flick's Streamside Guide*, Art Flick noted more trout have probably fallen to the Light Cahill than any other dry fly pattern. This may not be true in the Smokies, but the Cahill certainly is effective. This yellowish dry is created by using light fox fur for the body, and dressing it with wings made from the flank feathers of a wood duck and a light ginger hackle. These are carried in sizes No.12 to No.18.

Thunderhead

I am the first to admit this North Carolina pattern is really a Wulff-style version of the Adams. I have seen it tied with kiptail, calf belly, and even opossum belly fur wings. A good argument can be made that southern fly-tyers were creating flies with hair wings before they were popularized by the legendary Lee Wulff. The Thunderhead is a highly visible, high riding, buoyant pattern that looks enough like the many things relished by Smoky Mountain trout to consistently draw strikes six days out of seven. (Even the Lord rested on the seventh day.)

Yallarhammar

Another Smoky Mountains fly-fishing favorite of controversial origins, the Yallarhammar is a wet fly/nymph pattern preferred by many old-timers. The reasons are simple: the Yallarhammar is a consistent producer, particularly between late spring and early autumn. Its goldish-yellow color effectively mimics a variety of stonefly nymphs and caddis fly pupa found in these waters. These flies are carried in weighted and unweighted versions, sizes No.10 to No.16. Of course "real" Yallarhammar flies hackled with split wing feathers from protected yellowhammers (yellow-shafted woodpeckers) are no longer legal in the Great Smoky Mountains National Park, as these birds are a protected species. Fortunately, in recent years many fly-tyers in the region have developed techniques for dyeing legal plumage to match that of a yellowhammer.

Royal Wulff

The first dry fly that consistently produced for me in the national park was a Royal Coachman. These were fished religiously until I discovered the Royal Wulff, a hairwing version of this fly that is more buoyant and visible than the Royal Coachman. Each of these patterns feature a metallic-green peacock herl body banded in the middle with red floss, and dressed with a brown hackle. The Royal Wulff features hairwings made from kiptail. These are carried in sizes No.12 to No.18.

The Royal Wulff is a bona fide "prospecting" fly that mimics nothing that has ever emerged from these streams, or for that matter ever found its way to the Smokies, save on the end of a tippet. Still, trout seem to love the buggy outline of a Royal Wulff. I like them because they are easy to see in the churning waters of the park. An interesting variation of the Royal Wulff is the Tennessee Wulff, where an unknown fly-tyer substituted green floss for the red in banding the midsection of the body of the fly. The Humpy, which really is nothing more than a Royal Wulff with a deer-hair body, as well as the BKT Humpy, developed by Gary Williams, are also traffic prospecting patterns.

Hare's Ear Nymph

One of the oldest patterns used by fly-fishermen throughout the world, the Hare's Ear Nymph is a true "generalist" not tied to imitate anything in particular. In its smallest sizes, it resembles a small mayfly nymph, midge pupa, or even a caddis fly larvae. In larger sizes, the Hare's Ear Nymph effectively imitates larger mayfly, stonefly, and hellgrammite nymphs. These are carried in sizes No.10 to No.20. Variations worthy of note are the Gold Ribbed Hare's Ear Nymph, and the Beadhead, a version of this old pattern featuring a small gold bead secured behind the eye of the hook. The latter can be very effective in the Smokies.

Dave's Hopper

Of the many dry fly patterns tied to imitate the locally abundant *Melanoplus differentialis* or, as I grew up calling them, grasshopper, Dave's Hopper is tough to top. Created by noted fly-tying guru, Dave Whitlock, this pattern is rarely passed up by trout between late May and late October. If you have not discovered the deadly effectiveness of 'hopper patterns when fly-fishing the waters of the Great Smoky Mountains National Park, by all means try one. Dave's Hopper and the North Carolina version, the MarMac Hopper, are particularly effective between mid-morning and late afternoon during hot weather, a time when most other popular patterns are not as good.

Little River Ant

The creation of noted fly-tyer Kirk Jenkins of Newport, Tennessee, this version of the black and cinnamon ant has a proven track record on park waters. Like the grasshopper and other terrestrial fly patterns, such as those imitating jassids and inchworms, ants are frequently used by trout in park waters. A well-formed, buoyant copy of the wood ants common to the Smokies, the Little River Ant is carried in sizes No.14 to No.18.

Tellico Nymph

One of the oldest fly patterns to have originated in the southern Appalachians, the Tellico Nymph was developed as early as the late 1900s in the Tellico River area south of the Great Smoky Mountains National Park. Old-timers made the body of the Tellico Nymph from everything ranging from yellow wool yarn to yellow fox belly fur. Ribbed with a strand of metallic green peacock herl, and given a back of the same plumage and a brown hackle dressing, this pattern effectively imitates a variety of subsurface insect life. Carried in sizes No.12 to No.18, the Tellico Nymph is tough to top between early spring and early June.

Humpy Hairwing

One of the most overlooked secrets to dry fly-fishing is tossing a fly that not only is highly buoyant, but also easy to watch as it makes its way along the glides of the stream. A pattern of relatively modern western origins, the Humpy Hairwing admirably fills both of these requirements, as well as one more—it catches trout very well. The body of the Humpy Hairwing is folded over deer hair (caribou or elk hair can be used), dressed with kiptail wings and a brown hackle. Carried in sizes No.12 to No.18, the Humpy Hairwing is a sure-fire favorite of half-blind oldsters, such as myself.

Elk Wing Caddis

Remarkably versatile and absolutely essential for anyone serious about catching trout in the Great Smoky Mountains National Park, the Elk Wing Caddis not only can be used to imitate emerged versions of many of the species of caddis flies found here, but a sizable number of the smaller stoneflies as well. Exceptionally buoyant, if not unsinkable, this durable dry comes in more variations than the old Creek Chub Bait Company "Pikie." The Elk Wing Caddis can be tied with blonde, medium, or dark elk hair. The pattern can be given a floss body of colors ranging from yellow, gold, and brown, to black, green, and orange. Originally tied to imitate a caddis fly, viewed from beneath this pattern is essentially indistinguishable from a surface-riding stonefly. The Elk Wing Caddis is carried in sizes No.10 to No.18.

Wooly Booger

This pattern, known as the Wooly Bugger virtually everywhere else in the world outside of the southern Appalachian highlands, is an astonishingly nondescript pattern. Still the Wooly Booger has an indisputable track record for not only taking big trout, especially bruiser browns, but hard-fighting smallmouth bass as well. Exceptionally versatile, the Wooly Booger can be used to imitate small crawdads, hellgrammites, damselflies, or even small fish. Presented like a streamer or a nymph, the Wooly Boogers are carried in olive, black, and brown in sizes No.4 to No.8.

Muddler Minnow

King of the streamer patterns used in the Great Smoky Mountains National Park, the Muddler Minnow and its close cousins, the Spuddler and Marabou Muddler, account for a lion's share of the big trout and bass caught by fly-fishermen here. Carried in sizes No.2 to No.4, Muddlers imitate a variety of fish on which predatory trout and bass forage. Local variations of this pattern include those tied with wild turkey wing feathers tipped with white, a favorite of Greg Ward of Rocky Top Outfitters in Pigeon Forge, Tennessee. Ben Craig, the region's best known fly-tyer, prefers using speckled wing feathers from domesticated, bronze-colored turkeys.

Orange Palmer

A relatively new pattern of uncertain origins (it is certain the pattern came from western North Carolina, but no fewer than three old-time tyers claim to have created the pattern as early as 1960), the Orange Palmer is aptly name for a fly created to match the orange caddis fly common to these streams. Featuring an orange floss (or orange wool) body, the fly is dressed with a brown hackle (palmered) and an elk hair wing. Carried in sizes No.10 to No.16, the Orange Palmer is effective from early spring through late autumn. It is a truly indispensable dry fly pattern.

Prince Nymph

Another highly versatile pattern fished in the Great Smoky Mountains National Park, the Prince Nymph is a great mayfly and small stonefly emerging nymph imitator. All of these flies feature metallic-green peacock herl bodies, but beyond that variations abound. Dubbing of various shades makes the Prince Nymph incredibly versatile. The outline of the white goose biot wing imparts the natural look of an emerging fly. I carry the Prince Nymph in sizes No.12 to No.18

Smoky Mountain Forkey Tail

A pattern introduced to me by my grandfather when teaching me to catch trout during the 1950s, he told me his father introduced him to the Smoky Mountain Forkey Tail (as well as the Yallarhammar) shortly after the First World War. This pattern uses wood duck wing feathers. A couple of decades ago, another noted fly-tyer, Kirk Jenkins, with whom I worked for years and bought my first fly tying vise from, tied the pattern with black crow feathers. Ungainly in appearance, it is reminiscent of the wet flies offered during the early years of this century by Pflueger, Paw Paw, Webber, and other tackle-making companies. The large black crow feather versions of the Smoky Mountain Forkey Tail (sizes No.10 to No.12) are excellent stonefly nymph imitators. Duck wing versions of this old pattern in sizes No.12 to No.16 are excellent imitators for mayfly nymphs, particularly the March brown nymphs that are preyed upon extensively by park trout during late winter and early spring.

Chapter 11

Terrestrials: Too Important to Overlook

A tremendous dependence by trout and bass on terrestrial insects for food is one of the most interesting tidbits about fly-fishing in the Great Smoky Mountains National Park. Beginning with the spring and through the summer months, and especially during autumn, land-dwelling insects are vitally important sources of food for these fish.

When the feeding attention of trout and bass is keyed on terrestrial insects, it is a magical time for fly-fishermen. Rarely are these streams more productive than when these fish are taking grasshoppers, ants, and other terrestrial insects during the days of summer. Granted, most of the time these waters are low and clear, which does little to help the efforts of the average angler. However, early in the morning, late in the evening, on rainy days or days when it rained the day before typically provide great fishing. Understanding what foods are most available to stream trout during this time is the secret to catching these fish during the hot weather months as well as most of autumn.

Between mid-summer and late autumn the trout in these streams rely less on their usual sources of nutrition, such as aquatic insects, than at any other time of year. This is for two reasons. One is the cyclic availability of aquatic insects. Beginning in early spring, hatches of may, stone, and caddis flies dominate trout feeding efforts. Members of these orders deposit most of their eggs in the streams between March and June to replenish their populations. It is not until late autumn that many of these hatch and become significant sources of food for what anglers refer to as "catchable-size-trout." This gap corresponds with the abundance of land, or terrestrial, insects during the summer.

Terrestrials become available to stream trout in a variety of ways, from simply jumping into water, as is often the case of a grasshopper, to falling from limbs and other greenery hanging over the water, as is the case with caterpillars and jassids. Other terrestrial insects that can fly, such as bees, Japanese beetles, and locusts, often find their way onto the surface of a stream. Generally, frequent late summer and early autumn rains wash a bounty of terrestrial insects into the water. At this time buggy, nondescript terrestrial fly patterns, such as the Wooly Worm, are deadly on these trout and bass.

Terrestrial insects provide easily sized, high quality food at a time when the fish might otherwise have to expend considerable effort chasing minnows or crayfish. There are few terrestrial insects stream trout will not gulp down with gusto, especially on medium-size to small streams where land critters play a key role in the daily diets of trout.

One of the most interesting things about terrestrial insects fly-fishermen should understand is that even when dead these insects always float. Nature protects terrestrials from soaking up water when they are alive by providing them with a non-porous body that is overlaid with wax. Terrestrials are essentially water-proof. It is not to say a trout will not nab a grasshopper you offer on a line weighted down with a split shot sinker. However, it is a fact that a trout is more accustomed to taking a 'hopper from the surface than beneath it.

Grasshoppers are to Smoky Mountains trout what a ribeye steak is to you or me. It is a tasty, substantial mouthful that does not come around frequently enough to pass up. Grasshoppers certain-ly are not the only major terrestrial that stream trout feed upon, but in many instances they are of primary concern to anglers. When grasshoppers are available in large quantities, trout watch for these ribeyes on the surface. Anyone who has ever found themselves on a quality trout stream armed with a few good grasshopper imita-tions at a time when these terrestrials are numerous knows what it is like to experience a little bit of heaven on earth.

Another terrestrial insect these trout often key in on is the jas-sid, or leafhopper. Related to the grasshopper, but much smaller, jassids commonly live in streamside grasses and other greenery. When fishing streams where you see trout dimpling the surface along the extreme edge of the water, odds are these fish are munching down jassids, although occasionally this will happen when wood ants are working near the water.

At this time of the season, stream trout must keep a sharp eye out for any possible source of food. Several summers ago, while fishing Panther Creek, I came upon a pool where a basketball-size hornet's nest hung over the tail of a pool. Apparently the hornets were cleaning house, as enough debris was hitting the water to attract three foot-long trout. Tying on a bee pattern dry fly, I caught two of the trout before the third wised up and left.

Late summer and early autumn trout depend on terrestrial insects to varying degrees. At food-rich streams such as Abrams Creek, where streamborne food is always available in large quantities, terrestrial patterns are often out-produced by patterns such as the Adams. However, in the most classic freestone streams of the park, terrestrials are vital sources of nutrition.

And there are many seasonal terrestrials that are easy to overlook. For example, when the sourwood worms are available in early summer, these whitish-colored morsels are relished by trout. The thin, bright green inchworms we often see suspended from trees are another often overlooked, but highly sought-after tidbit. When they are common, Japanese beetles can be imitated with great success by fly-fishermen. During summer and autumn, it is usually a big mistake not to have a supply of terrestrial fly patterns with you.

Fly-fishermen who have not discovered the effectiveness of late summer and early autumn terrestrial patterns will be astounded when trying these offerings. Fly catalogs boast many patterns designed to mimic grasshoppers, jassids, ants, beetles, grubs, and more. Grasshopper patterns are my personal favorite, with the old reliable Joe's Hopper being tough to top. Should you find yourself astream without a 'hopper pattern when you need one, you can push a Muddler Minnow into service. Dressed with a floatant, a Muddler Minnow is a pretty good grasshopper imitation.

When fly-fishing for trout in late summer and early autumn, ant patterns are also worth trying—they are the unsung heroes of this time of the year. Now is the time to periodically examine the contents of the stomachs of trout you catch. If they are feeding heavily on grasshoppers, the stiff legs of these creatures will be easily seen when the stomach is split. Ants, on the other hand, are not so easily discerned. Sometimes you will find complete or partial bodies of ants, but most of the time it is only a blackish, or sometimes reddish, blob in the stomach.

At this time of year ants are extremely common along trout streams. Although an ant is small, trout will always seize one when it becomes available. Ant patterns in black and red, in sizes No.10 to No.18, should always be carried when fly-fishing for trout during late summer and early autumn. My best results have occurred when concentrating only the edges of streams, but trout will take ant patterns just about anywhere they are offered during this time of year.

Ant patterns and just about all other terrestrial insect patterns are fished in much the same way dry fly patterns are presented. Exceptions are when fly-fishing along grassy edges, where many terrestrial insects typically fall into streams. Fantastic fly-fishing is often available along shallow runs by offering terrestrial fly patterns such as a leaf hopper or Japanese beetle within a foot or less of the bank of the stream.

One of the best things about fly-fishing using terrestrial patterns at this time of year is you do not have to be there when a hatch comes off. You don't even have to get up early to get in on prime fishing. The warmer it gets, the more active many species of terrestrial insects become. High noon fishing can often be high octane fishing, if stream flow levels are in your favor.

If you have not discovered how using the abundance of terrestrial insects can up your catches of stream trout during late summer and early autumn, you'll be pleasantly surprised. Trout that have grown large since spring are there for the taking.

Chapter 12

Caddis Flies

Remembering the first time I encountered a big hatch of caddis flies on a trout stream in the Great Smoky Mountains National Park is easy. From a young age I spent as much time with my dad as possible, splashing about in the trout streams of these mountains. How I managed to ignore so much of what occurred around me in those days is still a mystery. That changed some thirty years ago during a Memorial Day weekend. Rising well in advance of dawn, as was our custom, we made the eighty-mile trek to the south end of Cades Cove.

This is where Abrams Creek emerges from the ground after traveling almost three miles through a limestone depression. Whereas all of the other 600 miles of trout streams in the national park have a pH of 5.6 to 6.5, the short subterranean trip through limestone jolts Abrams Creek's pH to 7.8 to 8.5. Coupled with the fecal bacteria and other nutrients contributed by the many cattle grazing in the open fields of the cove, this particular stream is blessed with a rich aquatic culture unique to the freestone streams of the Appalachian Mountains.

All of this was unknown to us at the time, and had we known, it really would have made little impression on us. What we did know by the end of that Sunday afternoon was that we had stumbled upon something that was nothing short of marvelous. Sometime around eight o'clock that morning the behavior of the trout changed. Trout that were otherwise spooky and reticent became bold, if not hell-bent on gorging themselves. Even in our uneducated state, we knew something we had never seen before was unfolding before us. It was a caddis fly hatch of the highest order.

We had read about air-filling flights of emerging mayflies, and were aware of caddis flies. We knew the trout were darting about under the water snatching morsels. However, the two telltale signs of a grand hatch—duns riding on the surface to take flight, and

*Understanding the importance of caddis flies to Smoky
Mountains trout can help make this happen for you.*

trout methodically dimpling the surface while feeding on the emerging flies—were missing. What was not missing was torrid feeding by the rainbow trout crowding this medium-size trout stream.

On an average, we hooked and landed a trout every four or five casts, and missed strikes at least two out of three casts. Using tandem rigged nymphs; a Tellico Nymph and a Yallarhammar, on at least a dozen occasions I caught two trout at a time. On numerous other instances, I would be working a trout to my net only to see one and sometimes two other trout charge up to attempt taking the fly hooked in the jaw of the first trout. During the course of that day I had over a dozen flies shredded to the point they had to be retired —a fitting end for any feather-shrouded offering. I do not remember how many 'bows dad and I landed and released, but I recall losing count around noon at more than one hundred fish. This madness went on unabated until dark, when I finally stumbled out of the creek.

Looking back, that day changed my perception of trout fishing on the streams of the Great Smoky Mountains National Park. Only on a few other occasions have I encountered trout fishing of that caliber, even on virgin waters in the Arctic, or at north woods beaver ponds where brook trout are packed in and nearly starving. A creek in the park that normally gave up forty to fifty trout on a typical day, rewarded our efforts with several times its usual limit. Frankly, had someone told me so many trout were crowded into the pocket water of Abrams Creek that day, I would not have believed them.

Literature regarding fly-fishing for trout is so heavily loaded in the direction of mayflies, it is easy for unknowing anglers to overlook the importance of caddis flies. However, in the waters of the smokies, the caddis fly does not take a backseat to the more highly touted mayfly clans in the local food chain. In many ways may and caddis flies are very similar. Each breeds as a winged adult and lays its eggs in water. Upon hatching, the differences in these two aquatic insects are at their most evident.

Mayfly offspring begin life as a nymph, which resides beneath the surface, clinging to rocks and debris located along the bottom, or burrowed in the sand. Usually capable of limited swimming ability, mayfly nymphs live underwater for six to twelve months, and sometimes longer. During that time, they may shed their nymphal outer shell more than one time to accommodate growth. Upon reaching maturity, mayflies emerge to the surface as winged duns. Once airborne, the duns undergo a second metamorphosis, to become breeding adults. Adults return to the streams in great swarms to perform their famous mating dance.Unable to feed because they have no mouth, adult mayflies mate, and they fall spent on the surface of the water, where waiting trout seize these protein-rich morsels thus completing their life cycle.

Caddis flies also begin life as waterborne sub-adult. Rather than being nymphs, though, caddis fly offspring are what biologists refer to as pupa. Whereas a mayfly nymph is a well-armored creature complete with legs and most other visible attributes of an insect, a caddis fly pupa usually looks like a plump, soft little worm resembling a common grub. In His infinite wisdom though, the Creator endowed the caddis fly pupa with all of the tools needed not only to survive in the hostile surroundings of a trout stream, but also to prosper. Caddis fly pupa construct "houses" for themselves that protect them from most predators.

In Park waters some caddis fly houses are constructed of sticks and leaves, while others rely on tiny pebbles and even sand as home-building materials. Sticks, leaves, pebbles, and sand are held together by secretions produced by the caddis fly pupa. One large group of caddis flies in the park constructs net-like seines, which they use to capture their food.

Usually measuring around an inch long, you can find "stick-bait," as old-timers refer to the caddis fly pupa, still occupying their abodes, by turning over boulders and picking up the submerged sticks used by these creatures to secure their homes.

Mayflies and caddis flies emerge in a similar manner. Maximum reproduction is facilitated by peak emergences of ready-to-bred adult flies. Sledges, as adult caddis flies are called, rarely ride the surface as long as a mayfly dun. Emerging sledges skitter upstream along the surface in a rapid, erratic fashion. This makes them far more difficult for trout to nab than a stodgy dun who rides along the moving surface waiting for its waxy wings to dry sufficiently for it to become airborne. Many times, peak emergences of caddis flies are difficult to see, while peak emergences of mayflies are often more visible.

Trout in the Smokies tend to prey on caddis fly pupa just under the surface where these small aquatic insects struggle to shuck their pupal husk. These efforts to emerge as a winged adult often makes the caddis fly pupa highly vulnerable for several minutes, providing trout with easy pickings. However, except for an occasional dorsal or tail fin breaking the surface, spotting the darting movement of a trout helping itself to a mass emerging of the caddis fly pupa is the only other visible hints we are given.

Many angling scribes have long penned prose expounding how trout relish mayfly adults and nymphs. While I am not contending these fish are not extremely fond of these aquatic insects, experience has taught me the trout will ignore hatches of mayflies in preference for picking off the subsurface struggling caddis fly pupa. Insofar as trout are classic predators, that is, they prey on that which is most readily available to them, it appears that the abundance of emerging caddis flies is an important occurrence that trout fishermen need to understand.

Ironically, surface riding caddis fly patterns such as the Picket Fence, Elkwing Caddis, Orange Palmer, Royal Trude, Chuck Caddis, or Greenbriar Special series often produce more strikes when surface caddis fly activity is not especially brisk. Admittedly, these dry fly patterns do produce best at streams and rivers where caddis flies occupy a prominent position in the food chain, which accurately describes most of the waters of the Great Smoky Mountains National Park. However, in my opinion, many times current-riding caddis fly patterns serve as well as prospecting flies such as a Royal Coachman, as they do as a traditional hatch-matching imitator.

When it comes to fooling these trout during peak caddis fly emergence activity, wet flies and nymphs are without peer. Remarkably simple patterns such as the Tellico Nymph and Solomon's Pupa in sizes No.18 to No.10 can be used to effectively imitate most of the vast numbers of caddis fly emergers common to these waters. Most caddis fly emergers are either dark brown to blackish in late winter to very early spring; to pale cream, yellow, tan, or bright apple green, the latter being dominant a mid- to late summer color.

Caddis fly emergence imitators can usually be fished up or downstream, depending mostly on stream clarity and size. When fly-fishing smallish to medium-size, gin-clear mountain rivulets, cast upstream, and allow the current to deliver your offering. This technique requires mending your line to ensure a natural drift as well as the ability to efficiently set the hook when a strike occurs. Casting upstream is essential at small, clear streams where your presence upstream from trout facing into the current would foil your efforts.

When water is murky, or when on larger waters where more than 20 feet of line can be played out, fly-fishing downstream is not only equally effective, but far easier and more relaxed. Trolling is a fly-fishing technique wherein you simply stand upstream from a potentially productive run where a fly is either still-fished in the current, retrieved very slowly, or methodically jerked back and forth. Casting upstream to a ten o'clock position and quartering your fly across the current to a two o'clock position is another time-honored medium- to large-water caddis fly pupa imitator fly-fishing ploy.

Old-time Smoky Mountains stream trout fishermen are quick to point out you do not need to wait for subsurface activity among caddis fly pupa to catch lots of trout. In fact, as these fellows are found of saying, you don't even need a fly rod. Collecting and fishing with stickbait provides an angler with what is perhaps the single most deadly trout bait, as a few unhappy anglers who have been caught plucking them from the back sides of stream boulders in these "artificial only" waters have explained. In fact, it is not inaccurate to say that collecting a dozen stickbaits and freeing them from their houses can take longer than wrestling as many trout from a stream, but can give you remarkable fishing. However, resist the temptation. To be spotted just turning over rocks to "look at stickbait" can land you in hot water in the national park.

Odds are, if you are unfamiliar with these streams, the caddis fly is the most overlooked, yet key element in your favorite trout stream. Understanding these interesting members of the aquatic insect community will improve your odds of catching more and bigger trout.

Chapter 13

Weighted Fly-lines: Breaking the Surface for Success

One of the biggest secrets of fly-fishing in the Great Smoky Mountains National Park, as well as the lakes bordering much of the park, is getting your offering deep enough for it to be noticed by trout and bass. According to Bruce Richards of Scientific Anglers, a leading manufacturer of fly-lines and fly-fishing accessories, although it is often said that fish feed on the surface only 10 percent of the time, 80 percent of the fly-lines sold are float lines for dry fly-fishing. Granted, it is possible to fish subsurface with a floating line by using weighted (or sinking) flies, or even weighted leaders. However, the depth fly-fishermen can reach effectively in these streams and lakes is limited. This does not even take into consideration the difficulties everyone experiences when casting heavily-weighted flies and/or split shot. When fishing the streams and lakes of the Great Smokies, experienced anglers complement their floating lines with a full sinking line or a line with a sinking tip for those frequent occasions when fish cannot be coaxed to the top.

Many anglers do not have a good understanding of full sinking or sinking tip lines, and that hurts their effectiveness. The following sections explain how these lines are made; how they work; and how, where, and when they should be used.

Sinking Tip Lines

Sinking tip lines carry impressive advantages in fly-fishing for species beneath the surface. Usually sold under trade names like Wet Tip or Sink Tip, sinking tips are basically floating lines with weighted tips. There are a wide variety of sinking tip lines available, with the major differences being the length of the sinking tip and its density, which determines the sink rate. The tips can range from 4 to 20 feet long, and have densities that result in sink rates from 1.5 inches per second (i.p.s.) to 6.5 i.p.s.

Most sinking tip lines are made in a two-step process that applies one coating, floating or sinking, at a time. The coating for the sinking tip is formulated with a high-density filler, such as powdered tungsten (used by Scientific Anglers), in varying amounts to give the desired sink rate. For slow-sinking tips, little tungsten is used—for fast-sinking lines more is necessary.

The floating part of the line is formulated like any other floating line, with a low-density filler, such as 3M's glass microballoons, to ensure proper flotation on water. The result is a fly-line with a tip that sinks. That will carry an unweighted fly below the surface. For most anglers, especially those fishing waters with a current, a sinking tip line should be the first line to buy after a floating line.

As mentioned earlier, most anglers despise casting heavily-weighted flies or split-shot on their leader with their floating line. The extra weight upsets the balance designed into the line and leader system, and makes casting unpleasant, at best. Sinking tip lines make the extra weight in the fly or on the leader unnecessary and make casting easier.

Sinking tip lines are best used in moving water. When fishing streams, rivers, or tidal water, line control is essential. Being able to control the line allows the angler to properly place the fly. Because the floating part of a sinking tip line stays on the surface, it can be controlled by "mending," or repositioning the line with the rod. Naturally, the line follows the fly. By mending the line the fly can be made to swim enticingly, and be presented to a fish in a very convincing manner.

In these mountain lakes, while sinking tip lines can be used effectively, full sinking lines are best in most situations. Since the water is not moving, the ability to mend the line is not important. Usually getting the fly deeper is critical, and full sinking lines are more effective for fishing deeper.

Many different sinking tip lines are available—which one is best for your fishing situations? First, make sure the line you choose is the correct weight for your rod. You should purchase a line in the weight for which your rod is designed—don't buy a heavier or lighter line just because it sinks. The "weight" of lines represents their density, not their heaviness.

Next, you should choose the density of sink rate of the sinking tip. If the depth to be fished is less than three feet, a line with a slow 1.5 to 2.5 i.p.s. sinking tip should be used. For medium depths, from 3 to 5 feet, lines with a tip that sinks from 2.5 to 4.0 i.p.s. will work best. For depths beyond 5 feet, fast-sinking tips from 4.0 to 7.0 i.p.s. are needed. These recommendations assume average current speeds. If the current is slow, use a slower sinking tip—if it is especially fast, use a faster sinking tip.

The length of the sinking tip is determined by the size of the water to be fished and the depth. The tips on most lines are 10 to 15 feet long, an ideal length for many waters. Shorter tips work well on smaller waters and when maximum depths are not needed. Longer tips can be very effective on large, deep rivers.

Full Sinking Lines

Most southern Appalachian fly-fishermen have a floating line, which is primarily used when the trout and bass are feeding on the top. But a floating line has limitations when you fish more than a few feet below the surface. As their name suggests, full sinking lines sink their entire length. The line coatings are formulated with a high-density material, just like the tips of sinking tip lines, but there is no floating portion of the line.

Full sinking lines are best used in still waters such as lakes and ponds. Because the entire line sinks, full sinking lines will fish deeper and straighter than sinking tip lines. Since you cannot see the fish strike a fly when fishing with a sinking line, you must depend on feeling the strike. Sinking tip lines are not as sensitive as full sinking lines in lakes, because the angle between the floating and sinking sections of the line creates slack, which cushions the strike. Since there is no current to move the line, having the ability to control the line by mending a floating section is not needed.

Sinking lines come in a wide range of densities and sink rates. The slowest sinking lines are often called "intermediates" and fish effectively in water 1 to 3 feet deep. Faster sinking lines are usually rated by number, from one to six, with the higher-rated lines sinking faster. There is no industry standard requiring every fly-line manufacturer's rating system to be the same as others, so check the actual sink rates given on the package before deciding.

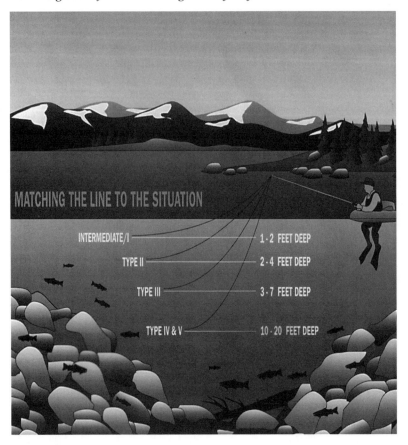

To determine what line is best for the depth you intend to fish, use the following guide, as further demonstrated in the illustration. It is based on 3M Scientific Anglers' lines—you may have to adjust for other fly-line brands.

DEPTH	LINE TYPE
1 to 3 feet	Intermediate/I
2 to 4 feet	Type II
4 to 8 feet	Type III
8 to 20 feet	Types IV and V

A rapidly retrieved line will not fish as deeply as one retrieved slowly, so if you know your retrieve rate you can adjust accordingly.

There is another type of sinking line that can greatly increase your fly-fishing success. Standard sinking lines sink in a "U" shape because of the way they are made. This "U" shape, also called the belly, puts slack in the line and can make strike detection more difficult in some situations. A relatively new type of sinking line with a "density compensated" coating, called Uniform Sink, virtually eliminates this problem and is the most sensitive sinking line made. If you will be fishing any flies that work best with a slow retrieve, a Uniform Sink line can really make the difference.

Although floating lines will probably continue to be first choice for most Smoky Mountains fly-fishermen, there are many days when a floating line just cannot effectively present a fly where the fish are feeding. For fishing in moving water on those days, a sinking tip line can be the key to success. In Fontana and Finger Lakes, a full sinking line, especially if it is a Uniform Sink line, can be the difference between a fishless outing and a day to remember.

Chapter 14

Bases of Operations

Of the eight to nine million people who annually visit the Great Smoky Mountains National Park, approximately 40 percent enter the park by way of Gatlinburg, approximately 23 percent by way of Cherokee, and approximately 15 percent by Townsend. Most stay in or near these locales or at Fontana Village Resort on the south shore of Fontana Lake. There are streams within minutes of each of these four major tourist stops.

GATLINBURG: The West Prong of the Little Pigeon River flows through the heart of the busy resort area. It offers excellent rainbow and brown trout fishing. Greenbriar River (the Middle Prong of the Little Pigeon River) is located 6 miles east of Gatlinburg off TN 73. This beautiful rivulet offers mediocre fishing for rainbow and brown trout. Little River, located 6 miles from Gatlinburg by way of the Little River Road (formerly TN 73), offers good rainbow and brown trout fishing. Abrams Creek, one of the better streams in the park, is easily accessible from the Cades Cove area, located 30 miles from Gatlinburg.

CHEROKEE: The Oconaluftee River and Raven Fork flow together just upstream from this picturesque town. Both of these fine streams offer very good fishing. The Transmountain Highway (formerly US 441) follows alongside the Oconaluftee, offering excellent access. Raven Fork is accessible upstream from the park boundary by trail only. Deep Creek, which flows out of the park near Bryson City, is also a sound bet for a day of good fishing.

FONTANA: Anglers wishing to sample the streams that flow into beautiful Fontana Lake can find no better base of operations than the Fontana Village Resort. Eagle, Hazel, Forney, and Chambers creeks all flow into Fontana Lake. The resort's marina will rent boats to cross the lake, or will caddy anglers across to these streams and pick them up later for a modest fee. The lake offers superb smallmouth, walleye, and musky fishing. More information is available from the Fontana Village Resort, Fontana Dam, NC 28733.

The Gatlinburg, Cherokee, and Townsend entrances to the Great Smoky Mountains National Park account for anywhere from 70 to 80 percent of the annual traffic. There are other areas which, though less well-known, can be equally sound choices.

COSBY: This entrance is popular, particularly among campers. From here you have excellent fishing opportunities at the nearby Greenbriar River (Middle Prong of the Little Pigeon River), the West Prong of the Little Pigeon (near Gatlinburg), Big Creek (off I-40 in North Carolina), and, of course, Little Cosby Creek at the campground.

BIG CREEK CAMPGROUND: Anglers staying here are among the most isolated, since waters outside the Big Creek drainage are a considerable distance away. The nearest are the Greenbriar River (the Middle Prong of the Little Pigeon River in Tennessee), and the Cataloochee Creek in North Carolina.

CATALOOCHE CREEK: Campers/anglers here are in much the same shape as those staying at the primitive campground at Big Creek. Big Creek is the only other trout stream within a reasonable driving distance of Cataloochee Creek.

BRYSON CITY: This town makes one of the finest trout fishing bases on the North Carolina side of the park. Deep Creek is only minutes from the Bryson City limits, and Noland Creek is only a short drive away on the unfinished North Shore Road. The Oconaluftee River is also nearby.

ABRAMS CREEK CAMPGROUND: This primitive campground makes an excellent base of operations for fishing not only the lower portion of Abrams and its tributary, Panther Creek, but also nearby Twenty Mile Creek and Eagle Creek, plus a number of smaller streams such as Tabcat Creek in North Carolina.

Fly Shop Information

When my Smoky Mountains Trout Fishing Guide first went to press in the early 1980s, there was not a decent fishing tackle shop that concentrated exclusively on the Smokies, or any guide services of note in the area. Today there are several. My personal favorite is Greg Ward's Rocky Top Outfitters, which has a no-nonsense, hard-core, catch-em-while-they're-hot" approach that fits my personality. Greg is one of the Smokies' top fly-fishing experts, and his guides are outstanding as well. Ward's shop and the other shops listed below offer solid advice on current hatches, where fishing is good, good selections of flies and other fly-fishing equipment, as well as guide service information.

Greg Ward
Rocky Top Outfitters
2721 Parkway
Pigeon Forge, TN 37863
(423) 429-3474

Jack Snapp
Old Smoky Outfitters
P.O. Box 488
Gatlinburg, TN 37738
(423) 430-1936

The Creel
6907 Kingston Pike
Knoxville, TN 37919
(423) 588-6159

One Feather Fly Shop
P.O. Box 553
Cherokee, NC 28719
(704) 497-3113

Little River Outfitter
7625 East Lamar
Alexander Parkway
Townsend, TN 37882
(423) 448-9459

Hunter Banks Company
29 Montford Ave.
Asheville, NC 28801
(704) 252-3005

License Requirements and Park Fishing Regulations

Either a North Carolina or Tennessee license entitles the angler to fish anywhere within the park boundaries.

Copies of current fishing regulations may be obtained at the Sugarlands Visitors Center, located 2 miles south of Gatlinburg in the park, or by writing the Superintendent of the Great Smoky Mountains National Park, Gatlinburg, TN 37738.

River and Creek Systems of the Smoky Mountains National Park

Chapter 15

Little River System

Little River

Size: Large
Fishing Pressure: Heavy
Fishing Quality: Good
Access: Little River Trail
Usgs Quads: Wear Cove, TN

The upper reaches of the Little River, particularly Fish Camp Prong, rank among my favorite fly-fishing destinations in the Great Smoky Mountains National Park. Drifting flies on the gentle glides found on this fair-size stream is about as much fun as man is entitled to have in this life.

Little River was the site of early pioneer settlements, and the hub of the largest logging operation ever carried out in the Smokies. The Little River Logging Company began cutting operations in 1901, which removed virtually every standing piece of timber by 1938. Those were wild times, because with the logging came a thing seldom seen in the Smokies—hard cash. Logging camps were the sites of numerous duels and a place where moonshine flowed free. The scars from this mammoth cutting are evident even today, although the slopes are gradually recovering their lost splendor.

All three species of trout now reproducing in the park can be found in the Little River system. The park's largest known brown trout, a hefty 16 pounder, was taken from the East Prong in 1979. Large brown trout in the 3 to 7 pound range are regularly taken from the deep pools of the Little River throughout the year. Yet despite the fact that trophy browns are often taken, rainbow trout are the most abundant. Rainbows that weigh 3 to 4 pounds are occasionally caught, particularly during the early spring and late

Little River is silly with nice-sized rainbow trout.

autumn, but the average rainbow will be 7 to 11 inches long. While brook trout can still be found in this system, most of the brookie water was closed to all fishing in 1975.

Fishing is good on Little River and its numerous feeder inlets. Fly-fishermen can expect to find sporadic hatches of mayflies and caddis flies, and hatches of large stoneflies occur in April and May. Large browns are often taken on a well-tied stonefly nymph pattern.

Anglers should note that during the warm summer months, the main stream and the East Prong of Little River become crowded with fun-seeking swimmers enjoying the stream's cool waters. Fishing becomes nearly impossible when such activity reaches its mid-afternoon peak. The best angling during this time of year is in the early morning and late evening.

A quick look at a map of the Smokies reveals the Little River system is one of the largest in the Smokies, bound on the south by Stateline Ridge, to the east by the Sugarland Mountains, and to the west by Anthony Ridge. There are numerous other ridges and spurs that cut through the Little River Basin. The main stream of

Little River is formed by three primary tributaries; the East Prong, the Middle Prong, and the West Prong. All three feeder streams have their own well-developed tributary networks that deserve the investigation of adventurous anglers.

East Prong of Little River

SIZE: Large

FISHING PRESSURE: Heavy

FISHING QUALITY: Very good, particularly for brown trout

ACCESS: Little River Road (formerly TN 73); all other access is limited to trail use.

USGS QUADS: Clingmans Dome, NC-TN; Wear Cove, TN; Silers Bald, NC-TN; Gatlinburg, TN

The East Prong of the Little River is often referred to simply as "Little River" by local anglers and in national park literature. Boulders the size of cabins are scattered along its course, plus an abundance of deep pools and long, swift runs. Several of these spots have romantic names the local anglers use to enhance the tales of a day's fishin': The Sinks, Metcalf Bottoms, the Junction Pool, and the Little River Gorge are all spots Tennessee trout fishermen know by heart. Other spots known only to local anglers are such places as Ole Elmo's Hole and Widow's Pool.

As this is one of the most heavily fished streams in the park, the trout here are often selective; a close inspection of your No.12 Coachman by an 18-incher will certainly put an extra shot of adrenaline into your system.

Mayfly and caddis fly hatches are sporadic, and often short-lived. Very few hatches in the Smokies compare with those of the East, though occasionally a lucky angler will stumble upon a surprisingly heavy emergence that entices the trout to feast.

Downstream from Metcalf Bottoms smallmouth and rock bass are relatively common. The largest rock bass I have seen caught in the Smokies, a 14-inch specimen landed by Vic Stewart of Morristown, Tennessee, was caught in the Junction Pool.

Upstream from the Elkmont Campground, Little River's character changes from that of a small river to a wild, cascading mountain stream. Fast pocket water, plunge pools, and beautiful

The lower reaches of Little River are often wide and slow.

scenery best describe this section. Beginning beneath Clingmans Dome, at an elevation of more than 5,000 feet, Little River quickly picks up water from other brooks as it rushes down the steep slope. Brook trout prosper in many tributaries (most were closed to all fishing in 1975). More than twenty-nine prongs of the Little River begin at more than 4,600 feet, with fifteen beginning at more than 5,000 feet. This is a diverse system with approximately fifty feeder streams draining its basin.

Access: The East Prong of the Little River is easily reached. Upstream from its confluence with the West Prong, for a distance of 14.5 miles, the stream is followed by the Little River Road (formerly TN 73), which winds alongside its junction with the Elkmont Road. Upstream from that point, the Elkmont Road follows the river 1.5 miles to a point just downstream from the Elkmont Campground, a developed area with 340 campsites. The Little River Truck Road, which was closed to automobile traffic in the early 1990s, is now a 1.5 mile foot and bicycle path.

Additional access to Little River is provided by the Little River Truck Road Trail, which begins at the end of the Little River Truck Road and follows upstream. At 2.8 miles, the trail arrives at the mouth of Huskey Branch, a speckle trout stream. At 3 miles, the trail arrives at the junction of the Cucumber Gap Trail. The Little River Truck Road Trail terminates at 4.2 miles at the confluence of Little River and Fish Camp Prong. Access to the main stream is by the Rough Creek Trail, which begins at the end of the Little River Truck Road Trail. The Rough Creek Trail arrives at the junction of Rough Creek and Little River at 4.7 miles (from the terminus of the Little River Truck Road). At this point, the Rough Creek Trail leaves the main stream to continue on alongside Rough Creek. The Rough Creek backcountry campsite (#24, capacity 14) is located near the junction of the two streams.

Farther upstream, access to Little River is offered by a maintained trail most commonly referred to as the Three Forks Trail. It begins at the junction of Rough Creek and Little River, and follows the main stream to 7.4 miles (from the terminus of the Little River Truck Road). The Three Forks backcountry campsite (#30, capacity 12) is located near this point. Grouse Creek flows into the main stream near the campsite; it is a fine brook trout stream.

An old, unmaintained path continues upstream alongside Little River (now only a small rill) to 7.9 miles, where the trail then leaves the main stream to continue on alongside Kuwahi Branch (8.4 miles) before ascending Stateline Ridge.

Jake's Creek

SIZE: Small
FISHING PRESSURE: Moderate to light
FISHING QUALITY: Fair
ACCESSS: Jake's Creek Road; Jake's Creek Trail
USGS QUADS: Gatlinburg, TN

Jake's Creek, a fairly good rainbow stream, flows into the main stream 200 yards downstream from the Stone Bridge at the upper end of the Elkmont Campground. It is reached by auto along the Jake's Creek Road from the Elkmont Summer Colony, upstream to .4 mile, the trailhead of the Jake's Creek Trail. The trail provides additional access to the stream for another 3 miles.

Fish Camp Prong

SIZE: Moderately small
FISHING PRESSURE: Closed, upstream from the 3,240-foot-elevation trail crossing
FISHING QUALITY: Good
ACCESS: Little River Truck Road
USGS QUADS: Silers Bald, NC-TN

Fish Camp Prong flows into the main stream 4.2 miles upstream from the terminus of the Little River Truck Road. Fish Camp Prong and its tributaries, Goshen Prong and Buckeye Prong, are noted brook trout streams. Access is provided by the Fish Camp Prong Trail, which begins near the mouth of Fish Camp Prong. At 3 miles the trail arrives at the Camp Rock backcountry campsite (#23, capacity 8). A short distance from the campsite, Goshen Prong flows into the main stream, and is reached from Goshen Prong Trail, which begins near the mouth of the stream and continues for 4.7 miles, before leaving the stream to ascend Stateline Ridge. The Fish Camp Prong Trail continues alongside the main stream 4.3 miles to the junction of Buckeye Gap Prong. The Lower Buckeye backcountry campsite (#25, capacity 8), a very nice fishing camp located above 3,500 feet in a beautiful forest of hemlocks, makes a wonderful spot to fry a meal of trout. There is no access farther upstream to the main stream of Fish Camp Prong. The Buckeye Gap Trail, which, incidentally is an unmaintained path, begins here, and follows tumbling Buckeye Gap Prong 1.5 miles to the stream's headwaters, before climbing Stateline Ridge.

Rough Creek

SIZE: Small
FISHING PRESSURE: Moderate
FISHING QUALITY: Good
ACCESS: Little River Truck Road
USGS QUADS: Clingmans Dome NC-TN; Silers Bald NC-TN

Rough Creek, which flows into the main stream of Little River 4.3 miles upstream from the trailhead of the Little River Truck

Road Trail, sports a combined population of rainbow and brook trout. It is reached via the Rough Creek Trail, which begins at the junction of Little River and Fish Camp Prong, then travels upstream .5 mile to the mouth of Rough Creek. The trail then follows Rough Creek 2 miles before leaving the stream.

Middle Prong of Little River

SIZE: Medium
FISHING PRESSURE: Moderately heavy
FISHING QUALITY: Very good; the lower reaches have yielded some impressive brown trout in recent years
ACCESS: Accessible by auto from its mouth
USGS QUADS: Thunderhead, NC-TN; Silers Bald, NC-TN; Wear Cove, TN

Seasoned Smokies anglers refer to the Middle Prong of the Little River as "Tremont." It has the reputation of producing some of the largest brown trout in the Park. A mammoth 12.5 pounder was wrestled from its shallow waters in July of 1980. Rainbow trout are predominant, though brook trout can still be found flourishing in the headwaters.

The confluence of Lynn Camp Prong and the Thunderhead Prong mark the starting point of Middle Prong. Other key tributaries include Spruce Flats Branch and Indian Flats Prong.

Access: Middle Prong is accessible to autos upstream from the mouth along the Tremont Road, located .2 mile from the Townsend "Y" on the Cades Cove Road (also known as the Laurel Creek Road).

The Tremont Road follows the stream, and at 2 miles the paved road ends and a gravel road (no longer regularly open to traffic during the fishing season) continues alongside the stream. At 3.5 miles, Spruce Flats Branch enters the main stream.

Spruce Flats Branch

SIZE: Small
FISHING PRESSURE: Moderate
FISHING QUALITY: Fair
ACCESS: 3.5 miles up from the mouth of Middle Prong
USGS QUADS: Wear Cove, TN

Spruce Flats Branch flows into the main stream of the Middle Prong 3.5 miles upstream from the mouth of the Middle Prong. It is a small stream, often difficult to fish, and receives a moderate amount of fishing pressure, particularly near its junction with the main stream. It is accessible via the Spruce Flats Trail, which begins near the mouth of the stream and continues upstream, offering good access to the headwaters.

Thunderhead Prong

SIZE: Small
FISHING PRESSURE: Fair
FISHING QUALITY: Fair to good
ACCESS: Defeat Ridge Trail
USGS QUADS: Thunderhead Mt., NC-TN

Thunderhead Prong flows from the slopes of Thunderhead Mountain. The stream sports a mixed population of brook and rainbow trout. Sams Creek, a nice tributary of Thunderhead Prong, offers excellent fishing to those seeking an escape from the crowds. The Defeat Ridge Trail begins at the mouth of Thunderhead Prong and follows the stream. At .5 mile the trail reaches the mouth of Sams Creek, and at 2.3 miles leaves the stream for the last time to ascend the ridge.

The upper reaches of Little River are seldom crowded with tubers or kayakers.

Lynn Camp Prong

SIZE: Small
FISHING PRESSURE: Moderate (closed upstream from junction
with Indian Flats Prong)
FISHING QUALITY: Good
ACCESS: Davis Ridge Trail
USGS QUADS: Thunderhead Mt., NC-TN; Silers Bald, NC-TN

Lynn Camp Prong is a fine little trout stream with an impressive tributary network. It boasts both rainbow and brook trout, though they are seldom more than 12 inches long. Tributaries of Lynn Camp Prong include Panther Creek, a nice rippling stream, and Indian Flats Prong, an isolated rivulet. The Davis Ridge Trail follows Lynn Camp Prong from its mouth, reaching the mouth of Panther Creek at 2.5 miles. The trail provides excellent access to Panther Creek 1 mile upstream before leaving the creek to climb Timber Ridge.

The Davis Ridge Trail continues upstream alongside Lynn Camp Prong, and at 3 miles reaches the confluence of Indian Flats

Prong. The Davis Ridge Trail (also known as the Indian Flats Trail) continues alongside beautiful Indian Flats Prong, which offers worthwhile fishing. At 4.7 miles the trail crosses the stream for the last time before ascending Davis Ridge.

West Prong Of Little River

SIZE: Medium
FISHING PRESSURE: Moderately light
FISHING QUALITY: Good
ACCESS: Auto access via the Cades Cove Road foot travel via West Prong Trail.
USGS QUADS: Wear Cove, TN; Cades Cove, NC-TN; Thunderhead Mt., NC-TN

Most anglers who fish the Smokies overlook the West Prong of Little River, yet the stream offers good trout fishing. The roadside portion of the West Prong and its tributary, Laurel Creek, receives the heaviest angling pressure, while the section that passes through the backcountry is relatively untouched. Most anglers bypass the West Prong in favor of more highly touted nearby streams such as Abrams Creek and Little River (the East Prong).

Rainbow trout have long dominated the main stream of the West Prong. A limited population of specs does exist in a few headwater streams. The West Prong, the smallest of the three prongs that form Little River, is bound by Defeat Ridge, Stateline Ridge, and Bote Mountain. Key tributaries include Laurel Creek and Bee Cove Creek.

Access: The West Prong is accessible upstream from its Junction with the East Prong by auto via the Cades Cove Road (also known as the Laurel Creek Road), which follows alongside 2 miles until the stream leaves the road.

Backcountry access is provided by the West Prong Trail (the trailhead is located at the Tremont Center), which crosses a ridge and at 1.7 miles reaches the banks of the West Prong, where the West Prong backcountry campsite (#18, capacity 8) is located. This is the trail's only contact with the West Prong.

Chapter 16

West Prong of the Little Pigeon River System

West Prong Of The Little Pigeon River

SIZE: Large to medium
FISHING PRESSURE: Moderate to surprisingly light
FISHING QUALITY: Very good to excellent
ACCESS: Newfound Gap Road
USGS QUADS: Mt. LeConte, NC-TN; Clingmans Dome, NC-TN; Gatlinburg, TN

For fly-fishermen short on time, but still looking for outstanding casting for trout and bass, the easily accessed West Prong of the Little Pigeon River is perfect. Despite the fact its main channel courses along a major throughway in the national park, it still offers excellent fly-fishing for trout and bass.

The West Prong of the Little Pigeon River has been the general over-mountain route of travelers for centuries. Long before white men cast their shadows on these mountains, Indians traveled to and fro across the crest of the ridge alongside this stream. During the early 1830s, the Cherokees built a toll road that ran along the same route as Road Prong (thus the branch gained its name). During the Civil War, both armies used the West Prong as a route through the rugged Smokies. Colonel Clingman, the military explorer of the Smokies, also used it as his route when ascending Clingmans Dome, once thought to be the highest point in the eastern United States.

The West Prong's watershed was thoroughly logged to the fir forest line. This area's farming and commerce were well developed. The forest has regained much of its lost stature, but open meadows crisscrossed with hand-laid stone fences can still be found.

Great fly-fishing is available just upstream from the Gatlingburg city limits.

The West Prong has one of the steepest descents of any stream in the Smokies, draining some of the highest mountains in the Appalachian range. Upon leaving the park, the stream flows through the center of Gatlinburg, then on to Sevierville, where it joins the Little Pigeon River. Primary tributaries to the West Prong include Dudley Creek, Roaring Fork, LeConte Creek, Walker Creek, and Road Prong. The confluence of Walker Creek and Road Prong is the beginning of the West Prong.

Anglers staying in Gatlinburg or Pigeon Forge will discover that the West Prong offers Smoky Mountain trout fishing with only a minimum amount of fuss. The quality of the fishing is surprisingly good despite its almost urban location. This stream abounds with a large number of 8- to 11-inch fish. Yet I've had more fish in the 16- to 18-inch class buzz my flies here than anywhere else in the park.

At one time, there was a rearing station at what is now the Chimney Tops Picnic Grounds. The stream annually received thousands of rainbow trout. The rainbows have done exceptionally well, reaching 3 to 4 pounds with regularity. Brook trout can still be found in several of the headwater streams, notably Road Prong.

Brown trout have invaded the lower stretches of the West Prong in recent years. Trophy browns are occasionally taken, but rainbows are by far the most numerous. The West Prong can be a treacherous little creek to get around on. Plunge pools are surrounded by deceptively slick huge gray boulders. In addition, the stream is often very swift and turbulent. Accordingly, some stretches seldom see one to two fishermen per week.

Smallmouth and rock bass are most common downstream from the Sugarland Rangers Headquarters. Look for these fish in the tails of large pools and along ledges.

Access: The West Prong of the Little Pigeon River is accessible by auto from Newfound Gap Road, which runs alongside the stream to about 4,500 feet. This road connects Gatlinburg, Tennessee, with Cherokee, North Carolina. There is ample roadside parking along the entire route, although traffic may at times be extremely heavy.

No maintained trails offer continuous access to the stream. The National Park Service has in recent years established a number of "quiet walkways" which lead to the stream. It is amazing how few anglers use these pathways. There are no backcountry primitive or developed campsites within the bounds of the West Prong of the Little Pigeon watershed.

Dudley Creek

SIZE: Small
FISHING PRESSURE: Light
FISHING QUALITY: Good to excellent
ACCESS: At the park boundary from TN 73
USGS QUADS: Mt. LeConte, NC-TN

Dudley Creek is a super little trout stream located only a short drive from Gatlinburg. This stream is fished only occasionally by visiting anglers, probably because of its relatively small size and somewhat obscure location. The stream has a plentiful population of rainbow trout in its lower reaches, and brook trout can still be found in the headwaters.

Novice anglers may find this a difficult stream to fish because of the dense flora. Laurel and rhododendron thickets shroud many fine pools from the reach of all but the most experienced casters. These dense, overgrown sections of Dudley Creek rarely see the fraudulent offerings of the fisherman.

Tributaries of Dudley Creek that warrant mention are Twin Creek and Little Dudley Creek.

Access: Auto access to Dudley Creek is possible via TN 73. The stream passes out of the Park approximately 1.8 miles east of Gatlinburg, and flows alongside the highway. There are no maintained trails inside the park, but an old National Park Service fire road provides excellent access to the stream for a short distance.

Roaring Fork

SIZE: Small
FISHING PRESSURE: Light to moderate
FISHING QUALITY: Excellent
ACCESS: Roaring Fork Motor Nature Trail, Trillium Gap Trail
USGS QUADS: Mt. LeConte, NC-TN

Roaring Fork has long been one of my favorite streams in the Smokies. It is located near the heart of Gatlinburg, yet despite this almost cosmopolitan locale, offers excellent rainbow and brook trout fishing.

Roaring Fork boasts the distinction of having the most drastic descent of any stream its size in the eastern United States. This fact accounts for the loud roar and almost continuous series of cascades and deep pools. These oxygen-rich waters support a prolific population of stoneflies. A well-tied stonefly nymph cast into its foaming pools will produce action.

Indian Camp Branch and Surry Branch are tributaries that offer good fishing.

Despite its closeness to the park's primary highway,
this stream offers great fishing and catches.

Access: Roaring Fork is accessible by auto from the Roaring Fork Motor Nature Trail, a one-way road. It is popular to park at the end of this road and walk in to fish, thus avoiding the drive around the loop.

The Trillium Gap Trail offers further access to the stream. It begins at the Grotto Falls parking area. At 1.5 miles it crosses the stream, and at 4.4 miles arrives at the headwaters of Surry Branch, a tributary of Roaring Fork.

LeConte Creek

SIZE: Small
FISHING PRESSURE: Moderate
FISHING QUALITY: Fair
ACCESS: Roaring Fork Motor Nature Trail, Rainbow Falls Trail
USGS QUADS: Mt. LeConte, NC-TN

LeConte Creek is located alongside one of the most popular foot and horse trails in the Smokies. This fact has not enhanced the fishing. Everywhere, hikers seem to grow like mushrooms. It is a nice little stream to fish, though privacy is elusive.

Access: Auto access to LeConte Creek is provided by the Roaring Fork Motor Nature Trail, which follows alongside the stream.

Trail access if provided by the Rainbow Falls Trail, which begins off the Cherokee Orchard Road at 4.3 miles, and follows the stream 2 miles to Rainbow Falls. The fishing quality upstream from the falls is poor.

Road Prong

SIZE: Small
FISHING PRESSURE: Moderate
FISHING QUALITY: Excellent
ACCESS: Newfound Gap Road; Road Prong Trail
USGS QUADS: Mt. LeConte, NC-TN; Clingmans Dome, NC-TN

Road Prong is one of the better streams forming the headwaters of West Prong. Rainbow trout occupy the lower levels of the stream. The upper reaches hold a fine population of frisky specs. A total of seven tributary prongs begin at an elevation of more than 4,800 feet.

Road Prong passes through the lovely Beech Flats area, considered one of the prettiest sections of the Smokies. There are a number of cascades and pools that can be easily fished by even a novice trouter.

Access: The confluence of Road Prong and Walker Camp Prong is 8.7 miles south of the Sugarlands Center, on Newfound Gap Road. There is no further auto access to the stream.

The Road Prong Trail offers access to the creek further upstream. It follows alongside the stream for 3.1 miles, to its headwaters.

Walker Camp Prong

SIZE: Small to medium
FISHING PRESSURE: Moderate
FISHING QUALITY: Poor
ACCESS: Newfound Gap Road; Alum Camp Trail
USGS QUADS: Mt. LeConte, NC-TN; Clingmans Dome, NC-TN

The confluence of Walker Camp Prong and Road Prong marks the beginning of the West Prong, which seems to have all the necessary qualities of a good trout stream. Unfortunately, the fishing is below par for this watershed.

The headwaters of Walker Camp Prong flow over a formation of acid-bearing shale known as the Anakeesta Formation. For eons Walker Camp Prong flowed over this formation, gradually leaching out and sealing the bulk of the exposed rock's acidic properties. The pH of Walker Camp Prong was always low, but the brook trout and other aquatic life forms found it bearable. When the National Park Service found it necessary to widen Newfound Gap Road alongside the path of the stream, the Anakeesta Formation was unwittingly cut into. The stream was then exposed to this freshly unearthed acid source. To make a bad situation worse, the silty-slatey Anakeesta was crushed into gravel and used as the bed for the new pavement. The aquatic life of this little stream has been damaged by this activity, and the effects will be felt for several lifetimes.

Rainbow trout can be taken in the main stream, and there is still a remnant population of brook trout in the headwaters of the main stream, but overall, fishing here is poor.

Alum Cave Creek, a tributary to Walker Camp Prong, offers mediocre angling for brook trout. It flows into the main stream at a point old-timers call "Grassy Place," a favorite camping spot for mountaineer anglers during pre-park days. Olin Watson, former president of the Smoky Mountains Historical Society, related an amusing story of a fishing trip that took place here around 1910. It seems a group of men from the flatlands decided to spend a few weeks up the West Prong doing a little fishin' and huntin'. At that time, specs were thick as gnats, and could easily be caught at any time. One evening, while the day's catch was frying, the jug of moonshine made a round or two around the fire. Now, 'shine often makes for some mighty tall talk, and that evening the subject turned to how many fish a man could eat. As the tale goes, one fellow ate around 80 specs before stopping. He managed to keep the fish down, but declined to join the rest of the angling party the next day!

Access: Walker Camp Prong begins 8.7 miles south of the Sugarland Center on Newfound Gap Road. This road offers excellent access to the stream to approximately 4,500 feet in elevation.

Alum Cave Creek flows into the main stream 1.3 miles upstream from the confluence of Walker Camp Prong and Road Prong. Further access is possible via the Alum Camp Trail, which begins at the mouth of the stream.

Chapter 17

Middle Prong of the Little Pigeon River System

Middle Prong Of The Little Pigeon River

SIZE: Large at the park boundary, smaller upstream
FISHING PRESSURE: Heavy
FISHING QUALITY: Fair, at its best in early spring
ACCESS: Greenbriar Road; Ramsey Prong Road Trail
USGS QUADS: Mt. LeConte, NC-TN; Mt. Guyot, NC-TN

If you are staying in the Gatlinburg/Pigeon Forge area, this is the place to go if you want to beat the crowds. This streamshed gets less pressure these days than it did when my first trout fishing guide book on park waters was published in 1981. That's remarkable, because angling success has improved on these waters.

The Middle Prong of the Little Pigeon River (locally referred to as the Middle Prong or Greenbriar Creek) is one of the more rugged watersheds. Prior to becoming part of a national park, Greenbriar Cove was a sparsely populated, primitive area. The terrain displays an ancient face. Wisely, the National Park Service chose not to develop this area, slowly phasing out camping and auto access. Partially logged in the 1900s, the area is well known for its virgin stands of huge trees and giant cherry.

The Greenbriar Creek watershed is located in the northwest section of the Park. Mt. LeConte, one of the highest peaks in the eastern United States, forms the boundary of the watershed to the south, with Mt. Guyot to the east. The primary tributaries are Porter's Creek, Ramsey Prong, Buck Fork, Eagle Rock Prong, and Chapman Prong.

The Greenbriar is a rough-and-tumble cascading creek, rushing over thousands of huge boulders, forming countless trout-holding

The upper reaches of this streamshed are packed with native brookies.

pools. Getting to these trout requires a bit of work, due to the extreme ruggedness of the terrain. But a day of fishing here is a sure-fire cure for insomnia.

Greenbriar Creek sports all three species of trout. Rainbows are the most abundant. Brown trout have established a foothold in the lower reaches as a result of stockings outside the park. In recent years the state of Tennessee has dramatically curtailed its brown trout stocking efforts downstream from the park, resulting in fewer catches of these large fish in the park. Brook trout still flourish in the majority of the headwater streams.

Greenbriar Creek is not a premium trout stream. This watershed has traditionally been prone to flash floods, which not only kill fish, but have a scouring effect on the bottom fauna.

Greenbriar Creek is at its best in early spring. There is a good population of stoneflies in this watershed, so stonefly imitations (basically nymphs) are always trout-getters. Nice hatches of small gray mayflies take place in the last few weeks of April, making for pretty fair fly-fishing.

The presence of smallmouth bass in the lower reaches of the main river is the well-kept secret of a handful of local anglers. Bronzebacks in excess of four pounds are routinely caught downstream from the mouth of Porter's Creek. Muddler Minnows and Dace-style streamers are the ticket for catching these bruisers.

Access: Greenbriar Creek flows under TN 73, 6 miles east of Gatlinburg. Entrance to the Park is possible by turning onto the Greenbriar Road at the concrete bridge.

The Greenbriar Road allows stream access by auto as far as the ranger station (.9 mile). This section of road is open year-round. During the fishing season, an additional 2.5 miles of gravel road alongside the stream are also open.

Further access to the main stream is possible via the Ramsey Prong Road Trail, which begins at the end of the road. It generally follows the stream, ending at the junction of Ramsey Prong (1.7 miles). There is no further access to the main stream.

Porter's Creek

SIZE: Medium
FISHING PRESSURE: Moderate
FISHING QUALITY: Good
ACCESS: Porter's Creek Road
USGS QUADS: Mt. LeConte, NC-TN; Mt. Guyot, NC-TN

Porter's Creek is gentle and easier going than the main stream. It would be difficult to be disappointed by a fishless day on this sparkling rivulet. The streamside flora is most engrossing.

Porter's Creek is primarily a rainbow trout stream, although there are still a few brook trout in the most remote headwater areas. The mouth of the stream is located 3.2 miles upstream from the Park boundary. Porter's Creek flows off the steep slopes of Mt. LeConte. Its principal tributaries are False Gap Prong, Long Branch, and Cannon Creek. False Gap Prong provides perhaps the best fishing of the three.

Access: Automobile access to Porter's Creek is possible using the Porter's Creek Road, which begins at the junction of Greenbriar Creek and Porter's Creek (Porter's Creek flows from the right). This gravel road follows upstream 1 mile to a large parking area.

The Porter's Creek Trail, which starts at the parking area, follows alongside the stream to its headwaters.

Ramsey Prong

SIZE: Small
FISHING PRESSURE: Moderately light
FISHING QUALITY: Fair
ACCESS: Ramsey Cascades Trail
USGS QUADS: Mt. Guyot, NC-TN

The headwaters of this little stream begin at an elevation of around 6,200 feet. It is a nice little brook trout stream. The only drawback is the occasionally crowded trail conditions. Fishing above the cascades is poor and not worth the effort.

Access: The Ramsey Cascades Trail provides access up to the cascades (2.5 miles). There are no maintained trails upstream from that point.

Buck Fork

SIZE: Small
FISHING PRESSURE: Closed
FISHING QUALITY: Good, particularly in late summer
ACCESS: Remote
USGS QUADS: Mt. Guyot, NC-TN

Buck Fork is a brook trout stream. Eight of the stream's prongs begin at an elevation of more than 5,000 feet. Fishing all day up this stream was like spending a day in Maine. Towering fir and spruce shade the sun's rays, as the crystal-clear creek tumbles over moss-encrusted boulders into foaming pools. The closure of this stream in 1975 was sorely felt.

Access: The mouth of Buck Fork is located .7 miles from the terminus of the Ramsey Prong Road Trail. Note: It is rough going to the mouth of the stream.

Eagle Rock Creek

SIZE: Small
FISHING PRESSURE: Closed
FISHING QUALITY: Good
ACCESS: Remote
USGS QUADS: Mt. Guyot, NC-TN

Eagle Rock Creek was a favorite haunt of mountain men during the pre-park era. It was a good brook trout stream. Nine feeder streams begin at an elevation of more than 4,500 feet. Eagle Rock Creek flows into the main stream from the right 1 mile upstream from the terminus of the Ramsey Road Trail. There are no access trails.

Chapman Prong

SIZE: Small
FISHING PRESSURE: Moderately light
FISHING QUALITY: Fairly good, at its best in late summer
ACCESS: Remote
USGS QUADS: Mt. LeConte, NC-TN

The confluence of Chapman Prong and Lost Creek forms the starting point of the Middle Prong of the Little Pigeon River. Chapman Prong offers fairly good fishing for speckle trout. The trout here are small, but scrappy and very colorful.

Streams such as this are at their best on rainy days during the hot summer months. A shower starts trout feeding. Ant patterns are lethal during such times.

Access: Chapman Prong is in one of the more remote sections of the Smokies. The stream's mouth is located 1.6 miles upstream from the terminus of the Ramsey Road Trail.

Chapter 18

Big Creek System

Big Creek

SIZE: Large
FISHING PRESSURE: Moderate
FISHING QUALITY: Fair
ACCESS: State Road 1332; Big Creek Trail
USGS QUADS: Waterville, NC-TN; Luftee Knob, NC-TN

Perhaps the streamshed that is visited the least by non- local anglers, Big Creek offers mixed bag fishing with trout in all waters, and smallmouth bass in the lower reaches downstream from the campground.

Big Creek is without a doubt one of the most beautiful streams in the Smokies. I have found that even on fishless days it is hard to leave this stream unfulfilled. The stream cascades down the mountain over massive gray boulders, forming deep plunge pools, slows momentarily, then rushes on to the next stop. An added attraction is the fascinating varieties of moss and lichen one finds attached to scores of streamside boulders.

Big Creek is located in the northernmost section of the Smokies. It is bound by Mt. Cammeree, Mt. Sterling, and Mt. Guyot, and flows into the Pigeon River. Primary tributaries include Swallow Fork, Gunter Fork, Yellow Creek, and Deer Creek.

The Big Creek watershed was thoroughly logged between 1909 and 1918, but under the protection of the National Park Service the forest has regained much of its original beauty. Further development has been halted, and some access and facilities have been curtailed in recent years. Despite these efforts, however, this is a popular area due to its proximity to I-40. The quality of fishing on Big Creek does not quite match the scenery. Most of the fish are

*Big Creek is one of the roughest places to fish in
the Great Smoky Mountains National Park.*

small (5 to 8 inches), because Big Creek is not an exceptionally fertile stream capable of maintaining a population of trophy-size trout. Anglers should also note that the terrain surrounding Big Creek is rugged, so getting about is strenuous, and can be dangerous if care is not taken.

Access: Big Creek is accessible by auto, by way of I-40 at the Waterville exit (No. 451). Cross the Pigeon River (locally referred to as the "Dead Pigeon") and turn left. The entrance to the park is approximately 2 miles away. From the park boundary, a gravel road follows upstream .2 mil to the Big Creek Ranger Station. The stream is located 100 to 200 yards from the road most of the time. This road continues on to the Big Creek Primitive Campground (.5 mile), the end of the auto trail.

The Big Creek Trail provides further access to the stream. It begins off the gravel road a few hundred feet from the campground, and from that point follows alongside the stream, offering fair to good access to anglers. At 5.2 miles the trail reaches the junction of Swallow Fork, and at 5.6 miles arrives at the Walnut Bottoms backcountry campsite (#37, capacity 20). Walnut Bottoms is a superb fishing camp located on a flat, tree-covered area. This site allows easy exploration of several feeder streams flowing into the main stream nearby, and is the only backcountry campsite in the Big Creek basin. Walnut Bottoms is also the end of the Big Creek Trail. The Yellow Creek Trail begins at Walnut Bottoms, and runs alongside Big Creek. At 6.3 miles (from the Big Creek Campground), the Yellow Creek Trail arrives at the junction of Gunter Fork, the starting point of the Gunter Fork Trail. Old maps of the Smokies refer to Big Creek upstream from this point as Mt. Guyot Creek, a name infrequently used today.

At 9 miles, the stream reaches the junction of Yellow Creek. There is no maintained trail access to the upper main stream. Deer Creek flows into the main stream at 9.6 miles.

Swallow Fork

SIZE: Small
FISHING PRESSURE: Moderate
FISHING QUALITY: Fair, at its best in mid-summer
ACCESS: Swallow Fork Trail
USGS QUADS: Luftee Knob, NC-TN

Swallow Fork is the first significant tributary encountered while traveling up Big Creek. It flows into the main stream 5.2 miles above the campground. This stream has a combination of rainbow and brook trout. John Mack Creek and McGinty Creek, tributaries of Swallow Fork, offer good brook trout fishing. A total of seven prongs begin at an altitude of more than 4,400 feet. Swallow Fork is a lovely little stream, well known for its canopy of impressive hemlocks, plus scenic waterfalls that roar like never-ceasing lions.

Access: The Swallow Fork Trail begins near the mouth of the stream, and follows upstream 2.5 miles before leaving the stream to ascend Pretty Hollow Gap.

Gunter Fork

SIZE: Small
FISHING PRESSURE: Light
FISHING QUALITY: Fair
ACCESS: Gunter Fork Trail
USGS QUADS: Luftee Knob, NC-TN

Located 6.3 miles above campsite, Gunter Fork flows through some of the most beautiful forests in the Park, and could be termed by anglers as the perfect size trout stream, because it is large enough to allow comfortable backcast room for the average fly-fisherman, and small enough to cross at will.

Gunter Fork sports both rainbow and brook trout in its numerous pools and little "pockets." Fishing on this stream reaches its peak during the last weeks of May.

Access: The Gunter Fork Trail provides good access to the stream, beginning at Walnut Bottoms and running concurrently with the Yellow Creek Trail for .5 mile to the mouth of Gunter Fork, where it then turns upstream alongside Gunter Fork for 2 miles before parting company.

Yellow Creek

SIZE: Small
FISHING PRESSURE: Closed
FISHING QUALITY: Good, the hot summer months are usually productive
ACCESS: Yellow Creek Trail
USGS QUADS: Luftee Knob, NC-TN

Before it was necessary to close Yellow Creek due to the precarious status of the brook trout in the park's waters, this was one of the most popular speckle trout streams in the Smokies.

The old mountain men of the Cosby area were extremely fond of crossing the mountains from Tennessee and descending along-side this stream with a cane pole and a can of red worms. For these rural farmers, late summer was the time to "make camp" in the mountains, sometimes for weeks, until their crops were ready for harvest. Nightly, great fish fries were held, in which hundreds of speckle trout were consumed, and jars of moonshine were passed around the fire. Those were the days!

Access: Yellow Creek is accessible at its confluence with Big Creek from the Yellow Creek Trail. There is no maintained trail that lends further access to the stream.

Deer Creek

SIZE: Small
FISHING PRESSURE: Closed
FISHING QUALITY: Fair
ACCESS: Remote
USGS QUADS: Luftee Knob, NC-TN

Deer Creek is a remote brook trout stream. My only experience on this stream involved a meeting with a large black bear. I came face-to-face with the bruin as I haphazardly rounded a lush rhodo-dendron bush. He was equally startled, but appeared to maintain better bladder control through the entire ordeal. Since that time, I have stayed away from this productive little stream.

Access: There are no trails to this stream. Its mouth is located .6 mile upstream from the junction of Yellow Creek and Big Creek.

Chapter 19

Cataloochee Creek System

Cataloochee Creek

SIZE: Large
FISHING PRESSURE: Moderate to light
FISHING QUALITY: Excellent; particularly good early and late in the season
ACCESS: New Cataloochee Road;
USGS QUADS: Dellwood, NC; Cove Creek Gap, NC; Bunches Bald, NC; Luftee Knob, NC

It took considerable soul-searching on my part before I decided to include this stream. It is so quiet and peaceful there, I almost did not want to let other fly-fishermen in on its outstanding trout and bass angling secrets.

The Cataloochee Valley lies in one of the most remote sections of the Great Smoky Mountains National Park, and is often referred to as the "Forgotten Far East."

Located off the established tourist path, Cataloochee has limited facilities—a ranger station and a primitive campground (28 campsites, located alongside the stream)—but a well-developed trail system. The Cataloochee Primitive Campground makes an ideal base camp for anglers wishing to sample Cataloochee's smorgasbord of trout streams.

The Cataloochee system is more like the combination of four separate streams, which converge within a relatively short distance within the cove. The main stream flows 7 to 8 miles within the park, before leaving to later empty into Walters Lake, an impoundment of the Pigeon River.

The main stream of Cataloochee Creek and a number of its tributaries flow through open fields and dales, often laced by weath-

The Cataloochee Creek area is one of the most scenic in the park.

ered gray split-rail fences, an ever-present reminder of the sturdy farmers who toiled in this green cove in past times. Many local streams are named after families who once resided here. Reunions of old Cataloochee families, held here every August, unite four to five hundred former residents and their descendents; a human heritage that bonds these mountains to the present.

This pastoral stream is not nearly so rough-and-tumble as are the majority of waterways in the Smokies. Anglers from upstate New York will feel quite at home here; the stream has a generous helping of long, slick runs, perfect for floating a sparsely dressed dry fly. Once discovered, Cataloochee becomes a personal Mecca that provides an escape from the crowds and hurried lifestyle of the outside world.

The main stream of Cataloochee Creek is populated by a mixture of rainbow and brown trout, with trophies occasionally taken of each. Terrestrials such as jassids, grasshoppers, and several other seasonal land insects are extremely important to the diet of these trout, particularly where the stream flows past open fields. Once, while fishing below the campground, I was lucky enough to be on the stream while one of the fields was being mowed. With every pass of the mowing tractor, a wave of fleeing grasshoppers would spangle the surface of the creek. The Hip's Hopper I used that day accounted for more than fifty creel-size trout (both rainbow and brown) within a two-hour period (all were released). I would never venture into this valley without an assortment of terrestrial imitations.

The lower reaches of Cataloochee Creek are alive with smallmouth bass in the 3- to 5-pound class. These fish are common in the stream to its mouth at Waterville Lake.

The Cataloochee Basin is bound by the Cataloochee Divide, Mt. Sterling Ridge, and the Balsam Mountains. Its key tributaries include Little Cataloochee Creek, Caldwell Fork, and Palmer Creek, all possessing well-developed tributary systems that deserve the attention of anglers.

Access: Getting to this remote area requires a long drive over a gravel road. Approaching from the west along I-40, take the Waterville exit (No. 451) and cross the Pigeon River. Turn left at the end of the bridge, and follow the paved road 2 miles to an intersection. Here, turn left onto a gravel road (formerly known as NC 284), and continue on to the Cataloochee Valley (approximately 23 miles).

Upon reaching the valley, the New Cataloochee Road follows alongside the stream for 3 miles, arriving at the campground. The confluence of Palmer Creek and Caldwell Fork is located a short distance upstream. The confluence of these two streams marks the starting point of Cataloochee Creek.

Full-bellied rainbow trout are common here.

Little Cataloochee Creek

SIZE: Medium to small
FISHING PRESSURE: Light
FISHING QUALITY: Good
ACCESS: Old NC 284; Little Cataloochee Creek Trail
USGS QUADS: Cove Creek Gap, NC

Little Cataloochee Creek is a miniature version of the main stream, not dominated by a long, all-encompassing single creek, but rather the result of several small streams converging within a short distance to form a medium-size trout stream. Little Cataloochee Creek's headwaters begin well above 5,000 feet, on the steep slopes of Mt. Sterling. Rainbow trout are most common in the lower and middle reaches of the stream, with brook trout still occupying the upper portions.

Tributaries of Little Cataloochee Creek which are of angling merit include Coggins Branch, Conrad Branch, and Andy Branch for rainbow trout, and Correll Branch and Woody Branch for brook trout.

Access: Old NC 284 travels alongside Little Cataloochee Creek upstream from its confluence with the main stream to .3 mile, where Correll Branch enters Little Cataloochee Creek. The road continues alongside Correll Branch for 3,600 feet, before leaving the stream.

Trail access to the main stream of Little Cataloochee Creek is available via the Little Cataloochee Creek Trail. To reach the trailhead, drive 4.5 miles past the intersection of Old NC 284 and the Cataloochee Road (in the direction of Mt. Sterling). At that point there is a sign which reads "Little Cataloochee Baptist Church, 2 miles." This is the starting point of the Little Cataloochee Creek Trail, which, for the first 1.5 miles, travels through a lovely forest setting. At 1.5 miles, the trail arrives at Little Cataloochee Creek (the only contact the trail has with the main stream), then travels on past Little Cataloochee Creek, and at 2.2 miles arrives at Coggins Branch. The trail follows Coggins Branch 2.6 miles before leaving the stream to climb Noland Gap.

Caldwell Fork

SIZE: Small
FISHING PRESSURE: Moderate near the campground; farther upstream the pressure decreases
FISHING QUALITY: Fish are small, but plentiful
ACCESS: Caldwell Fork Trail
USGS QUADS: Bunches Bald, NC; Dellwood, NC

The confluence of Caldwell Fork and Palmer Creek forms the starting point of Cataloochee Creek. Caldwell Fork is the smaller of the two streams, flowing off the Cataloochee Divide. It contains rainbow and brown trout in its lower reaches, and a remnant population of specs in a few headwater areas. Over ten prongs of this stream begin at more than 4,400 feet; however, the rainbow trout, the most abundant gamefish in the watershed, are the dominant species the entire length of the main stream. McKee Branch, a small tributary, maintains a population of brookies.

Caldwell Fork receives a moderate amount of fishing pressure immediately upstream from the campground. The quality of the fishing is good, but most of the fish are under creel size (5 to 8 inches).

Fishable tributaries of Caldwell Fork include McKee Branch, Big Bald Branch, and during the spring, Warm Cove Branch.

Access: The Caldwell Fork Trail follows the main stream from its confluence with Palmer Creek. The trailhead is located off the New Cataloochee Road near the mouth of the stream. Upstream at .8 mile, Den Branch flows into the main stream, the starting point of the Booger Man Trail, a loop that rejoins the Caldwell Fork Trail at 2.5 miles near the confluence of Snake Branch.

McKee Branch is located at 3 miles, and at 3.5 miles the trail arrives at the Caldwell Fork backcountry campsite (#41, capacity 10), located near a large open field known as the Deadening Fields. Anglers will find this section of the stream particularly suited for the use of hopper flies during the summer.

The trail continues upstream alongside Caldwell Fork. At 4.4 miles, Double Gap Branch enters the main stream. The Double Gap Trail offers access to Double Gap Branch, a very small branch of questionable fishing merit. Shortly after passing over Double Gap Branch, the trail becomes known as the Big Poplar Trail. At 5 miles it leaves the stream for the last time, to climb a small ridge, later terminating on the Rough Fork Trail.

Palmer Creek

SIZE: Medium
FISHING PRESSURE: Moderate to light
FISHING QUALITY: Very good to excellent
ACCESS: Palmer Creek Trail
USGS QUADS: Bunches Bald, NC: Luftee Knob, NC

The lower reaches of this watershed are home for tackle-busting smallmouth bass.

The main stream of Palmer Fork sports a mixture of rainbow and brook trout upstream from an elevation of 3,000 feet. Downstream from that point, it holds rainbow trout and an occasional wayward brown. Palmer Creek offers anglers very good trout fishing on a number of very beautiful and productive feeder streams; Rough Fork, Pretty Hollow Creek, Lost Bottom Creek, Beech Creek, and Falling Rock Creek all hold populations of brightly-hued speckle trout. Each has its own little tributary system that can be a delight to explore.

The springs that form Palmer Creek, once known as Indian Creek, begin on the sides of the Balsam Mountains at an elevation of more than 5,200 feet. From there, the stream picks up a steady flow of water from feeder streams as it tumbles down. It passes through former grassy glades and old homesites, before passing over the gentle terrain of the cove.

Access: The main stream of Palmer Creek is accessible by auto for 1.6 miles upstream from the campground. Upstream from the confluence of Rough Fork, the Palmer Creek Trail provides further access. The trailhead is located on the right side of Palmer Creek, 1.6 miles above the campground. It traces alongside the stream, and at 1.5 miles Pretty Hollow Creek flows into the main stream. This is also the site of the starting point for Pretty Hollow Gap Trail (see Pretty Hollow Creek following).

The Palmer Creek Trail continues alongside the main stream 2.6 miles, where Lost Bottom Creek enters. The confluence of Beech Creek and Falling Rock Creek is located at 3.1 miles. The combination of the two streams signals the beginning of Palmer Creek. The Palmer Creek Trail continues alongside Falling Rock Creek for a very short distance before leaving the stream.

Rough Fork

SIZE: Small
FISHING PRESSURE: Moderate
FISHING QUALITY: Good
ACCESS: Old Palmer Chapel Road; Rough Fork Trail
USGS QUADS: Bunches Bald, NC; Dellwood, NC; Cove Creek Gap, NC

Rough Fork flows into the main stream near the Palmer Creek Trail starting point. Rough Creek, once known as "Ugly Creek," offers good fishing for rainbow trout. It is accessible upstream from its mouth via the Old Palmer Chapel Road. The road continues upstream alongside Rough Fork for .9 mile, where it terminates. The Rough Fork Trail lends additional upstream access. The trailhead is located at the end of the road. At 2 miles, the trail arrives at the Big Hemlock backcountry campsite (#40, capacity 10), an excellent fishing camp. The trail continues upstream alongside Rough Fork only a short distance beyond the campsite.

Pretty Hollow Creek

SIZE: Small
FISHING PRESSURE: Moderate
FISHING QUALITY: Good
ACCESS: Pretty Hollow Gap Trail
USGS QUADS: Luftee Knob, NC-TN

Pretty Hollow Creek flows into the main stream 1.5 miles upstream from the trailhead of the Palmer Creek Trail. The Pretty Hollow Gap Trail follows the stream. The trail begins off the Palmer Creek Trail near the mouth of Pretty Hollow Creek, and at .2 mile arrives at the Pretty Hollow backcountry campsite (#39, capacity 20), also known as the Turkey Gorge Horse Camp. The trail continues upstream alongside the stream to the 3-mile mark, at which point it leaves the stream.

Chapter 20

Oconaluftee River System

Oconaluftee River

SIZE: Large
FISHING PRESSURE: Moderately heavy to heavy
FISHING QUALITY: Very good; the lower reaches of the stream are noted for producing trophy brown trout
ACCESS: Newfound Gap Road
USGS QUADS: Clingmans Dome, NC-TN; Mt. Guyot, NC-TN; Smokemont, NC-TN; Bunches Bald, NC; Luftee Knob, NC-TN

The Oconaluftee River is noted as a good brown trout stream, as well as the most overlooked, high-octane smallmouth bass fishery in the park. The stream is large, with an abundance of long, slow runs and deep pools. Browns exceeding 12 pounds have been wrestled from the crystalline waters of this river. Late fall is a favorite time for local anglers, who employ a wide variety of large stonefly nymphs to entice large browns. One fly I was shown, however, appeared to be an imitation of a large "tobacco worm." Constructed of raffia, the fly was dyed a deep green and tied on a No.4 long-shanked hook. I attempted to trade for one of the odd-looking flies, but its owner, Jim Mills, one of Cherokee's most successful brown trout fishermen, told me that upon receiving this pattern from an old mountain man years before, he had promised to never give a copy of the fly to anyone.

Despite the presence of brown trout in the Oconaluftee River, the adaptable rainbows are the primary trout of the watershed. Their eagerness to eat almost anytime food appears makes them favorites with average anglers. Brook trout, however, still prosper in a large number of headwater streams, particularly the Raven Fork system.

The Oconaluftee River is home to many big brown trout.

The Oconaluftee River is deeply rooted in the human history of the Great Smoky Mountains. The Smokies were the cultural heart of the Cherokee Nation, whose domain once extended from the mountains of northern Georgia throughout the entire southern Appalachians. Prior to contact with white settlers, the Cherokee civilization was considered to be the most advanced of any eastern North American Indians. Primarily farmers, their prowess in combat kept their neighbors in awe. The word "oconaluftee" in Cherokee means "by the river."

White settlers, attracted by the valley's fertile soil, first carved out homesteads in the 1790s. Later, during the mid-1830s, the federal government ordered the forced removal of all remaining Native Americans to the west of the Mississippi River. The result of this action inflicted on the Cherokees has been named the "Trail of Tears." A small band of Cherokees numbering about one thousand refused to obey the order and retreated to the more remote sections of the Smokies. Later, the survivors of those who refused to leave were able to purchase the land that we now know as the Qualla Reservation.

The Oconaluftee River watershed is located in the center of the Smokies on the North Carolina side of the park. The river proper is formed by the confluence of Beech Flats Prong and Kepart Prong. Other key tributaries include Raven Fork, Collins Creek, and Bradley Fork. Raven Fork and Bradley Fork both have exceptionally well-developed tributary networks that are of considerable interest to anglers.

Access: The park section of the main stream of the Oconaluftee River runs alongside the Newfound Gap Road (formerly US 441) for 10.4 miles, to the junction of Kepart Prong and Beech Flats Prong.

Raven Fork

SIZE: Medium
FISHING PRESSURE: Local anglers use this stream on a fairly regular basis, but overall it does not receive a great deal of pressure
FISHING QUALITY: Good
ACCESS: Remote
USGS QUADS: Smokemont, NC-TN; Mt. Guyot, NC-TN

Raven Fork is unique because it flows out of the park, then comes back in. Its headwaters begin beneath the fir-lined ridges of Balsam Mountain and Stateline Ridge. A total of eleven prongs of Raven Fork's main stream begin at an altitude of more than 5,000 feet, with the majority of these feeder streams merging above 4,200 feet.

This is a rugged area, a fact that helped protect the streamshed from the wholesale logging that hurt many of the watersheds in the Smokies. Choice market trees, such as walnut and cherry, were selectively removed from the region, yet much of the valley remained intact.

The stream's native brook trout were possibly spared because of two circumstances, including remoteness and fishing pressure;

fewer than two thousand rainbow trout were stocked in Raven Fork. In contrast, the neighboring Oconaluftee River received over a quarter of a million rainbows. It has been theorized that this has been a factor in explaining the population densities of the brook trout in the two adjacent streams. Raven Fork is one of the finest remaining brook trout waters in the southern Appalachians. It was named in honor of "Kalanu," one of the Cherokee Nation's most revered war chiefs, who resided along the banks of this stream.

Raven Fork enters the Qualla Reservation near the Big Cove area, then near its confluence with the Oconaluftee River flows back into the park. At the time of this writing, the regulation of that portion of Raven Fork in the park belongs to the Qualla Reservation. Directly upstream from the Qualla Reservation, Raven Fork flows through a section known as "The Gorge," which is considered to be one of the most rugged and primitive areas in the eastern United States. The water jets over weathered gray boulders, pausing in the depths of foaming pools before racing on. This section of the stream offers very good fishing, but it should never be attempted alone.

Access: The park portion of Raven Fork is one of the most remote areas in the entire Smokies. To reach Raven Fork, one must drive to the Cherokee Reservation. Big Cove Road, located off the Newfound Gap Road in Cherokee, is the easiest route. Follow Big Cove Road, which travels along scenic Raven Fork, about 9 miles to the junction of Raven Fork and Straight Fork. Big Cove Road continues upstream along Raven Fork, and Round Bottom Road enters from the left, leading up Straight Fork. Anglers wishing to follow Raven Fork should take Round Bottom Road, alongside Straight Fork, and at 1.2 miles pass through the park's boundary gate. At 2.5 miles, Round Bottom Road arrives at the trailhead of the Enloe Creek Trail.

The trail offers the easiest access to the upstream sections of Raven Fork. It travels for a short distance along sparkling Hyatt Creek, and at 2.7 miles arrives at the junction of the Raven Fork Trail. The Raven Fork Trail descends the ridge alongside the gushing waters of Enloe Creek to the banks of Raven Fork. Located at the junction of Enloe Creek and Raven Fork is the Enloe Creek backcountry campsite (#47, capacity 8), which is a super base camp for fishermen. It is nestled among some of the most spectacular cascades in the Smokies. Downstream from the campsite, Raven Fork is accessible by a path that roughly follows the stream.

Upstream from the campsite, the Raven Fork Trail winds along the swift waters of the stream. At 2.5 miles, the trail reaches the abandoned Big Pool backcountry campsite. The Right, Middle, and Left prongs of Raven Fork all merge here, forming a large, expansive pool, perfect for floating a dry fly. The trail leaves the stream to ascend Breakneck Ridge.

Straight Fork

SIZE: Small
FISHING PRESSURE: Light to moderate
FISHING QUALITY: Good
ACCESS: Round Bottoms Road
USGS QUADS: Luftee Knob, NC-TN

Straight Fork offers good trout fishing opportunities to those seeking a nice stream with limited road access. The stream holds both rainbow and brook trout. It is a decent-size trout stream, and fishing pressure is largely limited to local anglers. Round Bottom Road provides access to the stream, traveling 3.5 miles to the Round Bottom Picnic Grounds. There are no further maintained trails upstream from the picnic grounds. This is a tributary of Raven Fork, which is a tributary of the Oconaluftee River.

Couches Creek

SIZE: Small
FISHING PRESSURE: Moderate
FISHING QUALITY: Marginal
ACCESS: Remote
USGS QUADS: Smokemont, NC

Couches Creek is a small trout stream that is often overlooked for greener pastures elsewhere. It is picturesque, though scenery cannot entirely satisfy the desire to catch fish.

Fly-fishing is outstanding throughout the Oconaluftee watershed.

Bradley Fork

SIZE: Large at its junction with the Oconaluftee; smaller a
short distance upstream from that point
FISHING PRESSURE: Heavy
FISHING QUALITY: Excellent
ACCESS: Smokemont Campground Road; Bradley Fork Trail
USGS QUADS: Smokemont, NC; Mt. Guyot, NC-TN

Many North Carolina trout fishermen feel Bradley Fork is one of the better, if not the best, trout streams in the Smokies. It holds large brown trout and colorful rainbow trout in abundance, and sports an impressive population of native speckle trout. Its size permits relatively easy casting room for fly-fishermen and spinner enthusiasts alike. The stream annually produces mayfly hatches that capture the imagination of both anglers and trout. The lower reaches of the main stream are often crowded due to the stream's reputation and proximity to the most popular campground in the Smokies. Anglers willing to walk a couple of miles upstream will be rewarded with relief from the crowds and better fishing.

Bradley Fork's feeder streams offer good fishing, and are lovely. Among these outstanding rivulets are Chasteen Creek, Taywa Creek, Gulf Prong, and Chasm Prong. The main stream of Bradley Fork begins at the confluence of Gulf Prong and Chasm Prong. It is bound by the steep ridges of Richland Mountain and Hughes Ridge. Bradley Fork empties into the Oconaluftee 6.5 miles upstream from the park boundary, near the Smokemont campground. The Smokemont Campground has 180 campsites, and is often crowded.

Access: Bradley Fork is accessible from its mouth to the upper end of the Smokemont Campground by auto from the Smokemont Campground Road. Upstream from the campground, access is limited to horse and foot travel.

The Bradley Fork Trail, one of the finest in the Smokies, follows the stream to its headwaters. The trailhead is located at the end of the Smokemont campground. At 1.2 miles, you will find the confluence of Chasteen Creek, also the site of the well-developed Lower Chasteen backcountry campsite (N.P.S. #50, capacity 15) and the trailhead of Chasteen Creek Trail.

The Bradley Fork Trail continues on, and at 4.1 miles arrives at the junction of Taywa Creek, also the starting point of the Taywa Creek Trail. At 4.3 miles, the Bradley Fork Trail passes the junction of Tennessee Branch, a fishable little feeder stream, and at 5.2 miles arrives at the Cabin Flats backcountry campsite (#49, capacity 20). It is a nice spot, although it can become very muddy during certain times of the year.

Upstream from the campsite, the stream is reached via a path that is not maintained, which continues upstream alongside the stream. At 6.3 miles is the confluence of Gulf Prong and Chasm Prong. At this point, the path leaves the stream to ascend Balsam Ridge.

Chasteen Creek

SIZE: Small
FISHING PRESSURE: Moderately light
FISHING QUALITY: Good
ACCESS: Chasteen Creek Trail
USGS QUADS: Smokemont, NC-TN

Chasteen Creek flows into Bradley Fork 1.2 miles upstream from the Smokemont Campground. It offers good rainbow trout fishing. The Chasteen Creek Trail, which begins near the mouth of the stream, offers access to the stream. It runs alongside the creek and at 2.2 miles arrives at the Upper Chasteen backcountry campsite (#48, capacity 15). The trail continues on beside the creek for 3 miles before the stream becomes too small to fish.

Taywa Creek

SIZE: Small
FISHING PRESSURE: Light
FISHING QUALITY: Fair to good
ACCESS: Toywa Creek Trail
USGS QUADS: Smokemont, NC-TN

Taywa Creek is the second significant feeder flowing into Bradley Fork upstream from the Smokemont Campground. The lower reaches of Taywa Creek hold brightly-hued rainbow trout, while the headwaters are held by speckle trout. The creek is reached via the Taywa Creek Trail, which begins near the mouth of the stream, and follows alongside the stream for 1.5 miles.

Chasm Creek and Gulf Prong

SIZE: Both are very small
FISHING PRESSURE: Light
FISHING QUALITY: Good
ACCESS: Remote
USGS QUADS: Mt. Guyot, NC-TN

These two mountain rills merge to form the starting point of Bradley Fork. Both are primarily brook trout streams. The forest through which these aquatic gems flow is one of the loveliest in the Oconaluftee Valley. There are no maintained streamside trails offering access, but upstream progress via the streambed is usually possible.

Collins Creek

SIZE: Small
FISHING PRESSURE: Light
FISHING QUALITY: Very good
ACCESS: New Found Gap Road; Collins Creek Trail

Collins Creek is a surprising little mountain creek that offers very good fishing. I have never fished this stream without a nice fish taxing my tackle. I cannot say if this is an extraordinary stream or just a place where "lady luck" smiles on me.

An added bonus to fishing Collins Creek is the fact that it flows through a beautiful virgin forest upstream from the Newfound Gap Road. The lower reaches of the stream hold rainbow trout, while up in the headwaters brookies hold dominion.

Access: Collins Creek is reached the mouth of by auto from the Newfound Gap Road, 8.8 miles upstream from the park boundary. Immediately upstream from its mouth, Collins Creek passes through the Collins Creek Picnic Area. Beyond the picnic ground, access is limited to an unmaintained path, known as the Collins Creek Trail, for a distance of 2.6 miles.

Kephart Prong

SIZE: Small
FISHING PRESSURE: Moderately light
FISHING QUALITY: Fair
ACCESS: Kephart Prong Trail, Grassy Branch Trail, Sweet Heifer Creek Trail
USGS QUADS: Smokemont, NC: Mt. Guyot, NC-TN

Kephart Prong was named in honor of Horace Kephart, the Smokies' famous outdoor writer. There was once a trout and bass rearing station located alongside this stream during the early years of the National Park. Today, the stream offers anglers fair fishing for rainbows. The brookies have disappeared from this streamshed.

Access: Kephart Prong is accessible at its mouth by auto via the Newfound Gap Road, 10.4 miles upstream from the park boundary. The Kephart Prong Trail offers additional access to the stream. Its trailhead is located near the mouth of the stream, off the highway. It follows upstream alongside Kephart Prong, and at 2 miles arrives at the Kephart shelter (capacity 14). Here, the Kephart Prong Trail ends, and the Grassy Branch Trail and the Sweet Heifer Creek Trail begin. Both offer further access to tributaries of Kephart Prong.

Beech Flats Prong

SIZE: Small
FISHING PRESSURE: Moderate to light
FISHING QUALITY: Fair to somewhat poor
ACCESS: Newfound Gap Road
USGS QUADS: Smokemont, NC; Mt. Guyot, NC-TN

Beech Flats Prong is, in truth, the upstream extension of the main stream of the Oconaluftee River. It is a scenic little rivulet, though not a particularly outstanding trout stream. The stream flows over a formation of acid-bearing shale known as the Anakeesta Formation. For eons, Beech Flat Prong flowed over this formation, gradually leeching out and sealing the bulk of the exposed "hot" rocks' acidic properties. The pH of Beech Flats Prong was always low, but the brook trout and other aquatic life forms found it bearable, and prospered. When the National Park Service thought it necessary to widen Newfound Gap Road along-side the path of the stream, the Anakeesta Formation was unwit-tingly cut into. The stream was then exposed to this freshly-unearthed acid source. To make a bad situation worse, the Anakeesta was crushed into gravel, and used as the bed for the new pavement. The aquatic life of this little stream has been damaged by this act, and the effects will be felt for several lifetimes. Kanati Fork is a nice little tributary of Beech Flats Prong.

Access: The Newfound Gap Road follows alongside the route of Beech Flats Prong for 2.8 miles. Upstream from the highway's last contact with the stream, a National Park Service road parallels the stream to its headwaters.

Kanati Fork

SIZE: Very small
FISHING PRESSURE: Light
FISHING QUALITY: Very good
ACCESS: Kanati Fork Trail
USGS QUADS: Smokemont, NC-TN

Kanati Fork, a tributary of Beech Flats Prong, is a small stream often overlooked by anglers. It offers great fishing for native brook trout. "Kanati" is Cherokee meaning "lucky hunter." Anglers wishing to try their luck here should by all means use barbless hooks or crimp down the barbs of the flies used. Kanati Fork is accessible by auto at its mouth via the Newfound Gap Road. It enters the main stream 10.6 miles upstream from the park bound-ary. The Kanati Fork Trail lends access to the stream beyond that point. Its trailhead is located near the mouth of the stream, and provides fair access for a short distance. Kanati Fork flows into Beech Flats Prong, the headwaters of the Oconaluftee River.

Chapter 21

Deep Creek System

Deep Creek

SIZE: Large
FISHING PRESSURE: Moderately heavy near the Deep Creek campground, moderate in the backcountry
FISHING QUALITY: Very good
ACCESS: Deep Creek Road Trail
USGS QUADS: Bryson City, NC; Clingmans Dome, NC-TN

Few streams in the Great Smoky Mountains National Park have a richer fly-fishing tradition than Deep Creek. It is one of the more highly publicized streams in the Smokies. Trophy brown trout weighing more than 10 pounds have been wrestled from its emerald-green pools. Few things can compare with a 16-inch rainbow emptying the line from your reel as it flees down one of Deep Creek's swift runs.

Brook trout still flourish in the headwater streams. You will begin to encounter these aquatic jewels at an elevation of approximately 3,600 feet. It is good to carry several fly patterns tied on barbless hooks, or pliers for crimping down the barbs on your flies, when fishing the backcountry here. A safely returned brook trout has an excellent chance of survival, whereas an injured spec might never recover from an encounter with a barbed hook.

As is the case with virtually every large streamshed in the national park, the lower reaches of Deep Creek abound with seldom-cast-to smallmouth and rock bass. Smallies up to 5 pounds are caught here by the handful of local anglers aware of the presence of these spunky gamesters.

This valley was spared some of the wholesale destruction loggers levied on the majority of the watersheds of the Smokies. Deep Creek's rough terrain made getting the lumber out uneconomical,

Deep Creek was the favorite haunt of the legendary Mark Cathey.

although valuable species such as poplar, walnut, and cherry were selectively cut.

Deep Creek was the favorite haunt of Horace Kephart, the famous Bryson City resident and early advocate for the creation of a national park in the southern Appalachian highlands. Kephart made many trips up this stream, recording his experiences in his writing. This was also the favorite fishing spot of the mountaineer fishing guide Mark Cathey. Cathey guided numerous parties into this valley, and delighted in showing the elite anglers of the East his awesomely deadly "dance of the fly."

Much has been written about Cathey's legendary figure-eight, dancing fly act which he loved to perform for anglers from all over the world who visited his favorite stream. In his well-known book, *Hunting and Fishing in the Great Smokies*, Jim Gasque described the dance as follows:

> ". . . he (Cathey) jigged and danced his dry fly on the surface all about him without apparent effort to retrieve. He retrieved only when a fish was on, but that was frequent. It was a distinct departure from the conventional method of making the cast and allowing the fly to float down the current. . . "

> "He made the fly wobble and dance on the surface by an almost invisible wrist movement that kept the rod tip trembling and shaking constantly."

Clearly Mark Cathey and probably other anglers from the Great Smoky Mountains understood the deadly value of the currently popular notion of fishing a dry fly as a living insect. When in the vicinity of Bryson City, it is worth looking up Mark Cathey's tombstone, which reads, "Mark Cathey, beloved hunter and fisherman, was caught by the Gospel hook, just before the season closed for good."

Deep Creek is fortunate to possess a rich aquatic insect community. Mayfly hatches are heaviest during the early spring and late summer. In addition, Deep Creek is noted for its large population of stoneflies. The only drawback to fishing Deep Creek is the steady stream of tube-riding fun-seekers who systematically filter down the last mile or so of the stream. Deep Creek is bound by Thomas Ridge, Stateline Ridge, and the Noland Divide. Its principal tributaries are Indian Creek, Bridge Creek, Pole Road Creek, the Left Fork, Nettle Branch, Cherry Creek, Rocky Fork, and Sahlee Creek.

My personal favorite fly-fishing stretch at Deep Creek is Bumgardner Bend, a semi-remote section of the stream that requires just enough effort to visit to keep the faint of heart at bay.

Access: Deep Creek has auto access from the Deep Creek Campground, located south of Cherokee via US 19 through Bryson City (from Bryson City the route is well-marked). Access upstream from the campground is provided by the Deep Creek Road Trail. This auto trail begins at the campground, and terminates in 2.2 miles at the trailhead of Deep Creek Trail.

Smallmouth bass are an overlooked quarry
common to the lower reaches of Deep Creek.

The Deep Creek Hiking Trail follows intermittently alongside the stream, and at 2.6 miles (from the Deep Creek Campground) arrives at the Bumgardner Branch backcountry campsite (#60, capacity 10). This is a small campsite, located 100 feet from the stream. At 5.3 miles is the McCracken Branch backcountry campsite (#59, capacity 6), a popular fishing camp. At 5.5 miles is the Nicks Nest Branch backcountry campsite (#58, capacity 6), and at 6.1 miles is the Bryson Place backcountry campsite (#57, capacity 20). The Burnt Spruce backcountry campsite (#56, capacity 10) is located .3 mile upstream from the Bryson Place site.

Pole Road Creek is located at 7 miles, and is the site of the Pole Road backcountry campsite (#55, capacity 15), also the trailhead of the Pole Road Trail. At 7.4 miles the Left Fork of Deep Creek flows into the main stream, and at 8 miles is the Nettle Creek backcountry campsite (#54, capacity 8), a popular streamside camp. Beetree Creek joins the main stream at 8.4 miles, and at 10.4 miles the trail passes the Poke Patch backcountry campsite (#53, capacity 12). The confluence of Deep Creek and Rocky Fork is located at 11.6 miles, and at 12.5 miles is the junction of Sahlee Creek. The trail continues alongside the stream to 4,060 feet before ascending Thomas Ridge.

Indian Creek

SIZE: Medium
FISHING PRESSURE: Moderately heavy
FISHING QUALITY: Good
ACCESS: Indian Creek Trail; Deep Creek Campground
USGS QUADS: Bryson City, NC; Clingmans Dome, NC-TN

Indian Creek is a medium-size stream that offers good fishing. The headwaters of this stream lie tucked between the steep grades of Thomas Ridge and Sunkota Ridge.

Brown trout are occasionally landed in the extreme downstream portion of Indian Creek, although rainbows are the stream's dominant species. Brookies have all but vanished from the streamshed.

Indian Creek is a popular fishing spot, and the trail leading to the stream is often crowded with sightseers, who find the walk to Indian Falls irresistible.

Access: The mouth of the stream is located 2.2 miles from the campground. The Indian Creek Trail provides access to the stream. It follows alongside the stream to the falls, and at 4 miles leaves the stream. An unmaintained path provides further access to the stream.

Pole Road Creek

SIZE: Small
FISHING PRESSURE: Moderate
FISHING QUALITY: Very good
ACCESS: Pole Road Trail
USGS QUADS: Bryson City, NC; Clingmans Dome, NC-TN

Pole Road Creek is a small, but respectable, trout stream. The population is composed primarily of rainbows, but a fragile community of brook trout can be found in the headwaters. The trout in this stream are surprisingly wary of anglers.

Access: The Pole Road Trail provides access to Pole Road Creek. It begins at the mouth of the stream, which is located 7 miles upstream from the campground, after a ford of Deep Creek. The trail follows alongside the stream for 2 miles before leaving to ascend Sassafras Gap.

The Left Fork of Deep Creek

SIZE: Medium
FISHING PRESSURE: Moderate
FISHING QUALITY: Very good, at its best from late spring through early fall
ACCESS: Unmaintained Trail (see Access)
USGS QUADS: Clingmans Dome, NC-TN

The Left Fork is one of the largest tributaries in the Deep Creek watershed. The mouth of the stream (.4 mile upstream from the Pole Road trailhead) is sometimes difficult to locate from the Deep Creek Trail.

The lower reaches of the stream are dominated by rainbow trout. The headwaters support a good population of brookies. Five prongs of this stream begin at an elevation of more than 4,800 feet, and to most experienced Southern trout fishermen, that spells specs.

Noteworthy tributaries of the Left Fork are Bearpen Branch and Keg Drive Branch.

Access: The best method for reaching this stream is to fish upstream from Pole Road Creek to the mouth. The mouth of the stream is 7.4 miles upstream from the campground There is an old, unmaintained trail that follows the stream, but it is at times difficult to locate.

Beetree Creek

SIZE: Small
FISHING PRESSURE: Closed
FISHING QUALITY: Fair to poor
ACCESS: Remote; Deep Creek Campground
USGS QUADS: Clingmans Dome, NC-TN

Beetree Creek was once a productive brook trout stream. It is located in one of the loveliest coves in the Smokies. Massive poplars and hemlocks tower above the stream like eternal guardians. Unfortunately, in recent years, the quality of fishing on this stream has eroded, making it a poor choice.

Access: The mouth of the stream is located 8.4 miles upstream from the campground. The stream has no access trails.

Rocky Fork

SIZE: Small
FISHING PRESSURE: Moderate to light
FISHING QUALITY: Good
ACCESS: Remote; Deep Creek Campground
USGS QUADS: Clingmans Dome, NC-TN

Rocky Fork is a picturesque mountain brook. Tumbling cascades and cool, clear pools are an open invitation to fishermen. It has a combination of rainbow and brook trout at the mouth of the stream, but as one progresses upstream, it quickly becomes a purely brook trout residence.

This is one of the better brook trout streams that was not closed in 1975, but anglers should be forewarned that this is a backcountry stream, located in an fairly remote section of the park. When you decide to fish in such a place, you must depend on yourself. Should you be injured, it could be days, weeks, or even longer before another human being casts a shadow on your face.

Access: The mouth of the stream is located 11.6 miles from the campground; however, anglers should note that the distance from Newfound Gap is 2.8 miles. The stream has no access trails.

Sahlee Creek

SIZE: Small
FISHING PRESSURE: Closed
FISHING QUALITY: Good
ACCESS: Remote; Deep Creek Campground

Sahlee Creek suffers from being too easily reached from Newfound Gap. Partially as a result of this, the stream was closed to all fishing in 1975. A beautiful stream with an unusual number of deadfalls crisscrossing it, Sahlee Creek is a physically tiring stream to fish.

Access: The mouth of the stream is located 12.5 miles. upstream from the campground; however, anglers should note the distance from Newfound Gap is 1.9 miles USGS QUADS: Clingmans Dome, NC-TN. There are no streamside trails.

Chapter 22

Noland Creek System

Noland Creek

SIZE: Medium
FISHING PRESSURE: Moderate near the mouth of the stream, somewhat less intense farther upstream
FISHING QUALITY: Very good
ACCESS: North Shore Road, Noland Creek Trail
USGS QUADS: Clingmans Dome, NC-TN; Bryson City, NC-TN; Noland Creek, NC; Silers Bald, NC-TN

Designed for the stout of soul and body, this tough- to-get-around-on rivulet is one of the best-kept secrets in the Great Smoky Mountains National Park. It hosts all of the usual suspects, including trout and bass, which are present in good numbers and size.

The Noland Creek Valley seems to impart tranquillity and peace of mind. Most of Noland's headwater streams flow through stands of virgin forest, making fishing here a delight.

The overpowering beauty of this valley has not been forgotten by its former residents. The area's rural dwellers were reluctant to leave their homes when the park was created. Former landowners and their descendants frequently come here to fish and walk among the tall trees they refer to with misty eyes as the "old home-place."

During the pre-park era, the Noland Creek watershed was a remote farming community. The families living here in the hollows and coves of the valley supported themselves raising corn and cattle. Corn not needed for bread or winter cattle feed usually found its way through the copper lining of a still. Making mountain "corn likker," or moonshine, was not only an honored art in the mountains of the South, but a reliable source of hard cash. During lean

Crowds are never a problem at remote Noland Creek.

times, which were common in this area, it often helped put shoes on the children's feet.

At the turn of the century, the Noland Creek watershed was passed over by the logging operators who sprang on the Smokies like hungry wolves on the fold. There were selective cuttings of valuable market species, and clearing of tillable ground, but most of the ridge lines are still covered with virgin growth.

Fishing on Noland Creek is very good. In recent years, brown trout have established themselves in the lower sections of the main stream. Fly-fishermen using big stonefly nymph or stream-er pattern flies take occasional trophy browns from Noland Creek.

Rainbow trout are common from the mouth of the stream to about an elevation of 4,000 feet, and average 7 to 11 inches. But don't be too surprised by the surge of a 16-incher if you drop the right offering in the right spot at the right time.

Brook trout flourish in the headwaters of several streams. Anglers planning to fish the backcountry should make a point of bringing along flies tied on barbless hooks, or pliers for crimping down barbs.

Noland Creek is located in the southeast section of the Great Smoky Mountains National Park. It is one of the smallest major streams flowing out of the Smokies into Fontana Lake. It is bound by Forney Ridge, Stateline Ridge, and the Noland Divide. The principal tributaries of the main stream include Bearpen Branch, Mill Creek, Bald Branch, Salola Branch, and Clingmans Creek.

Access: Noland Creek flows into the Tuckasegee River branch of Fontana Lake. It is accessible by auto from North Shore Road (which can be reached via US 19 through Bryson City), which crosses the Noland Divide and reaches the stream at approximately 7 miles.

The Noland Creek Trail provides further stream access. The trailhead is located near the Noland Creek Bridge, off the highway. The trail travels alongside the stream, and arrives at the confluence of Bearpen Branch and the Bearpen Branch backcountry campsite (#65, capacity 8) at approximately 1.7 miles. The trail continues upstream and at 4 miles reaches the junction of Mill Creek in the Salola Valley, the site of the Mill Creek Horse Camp backcountry campsite (#64, capacity 20) and the trailhead of the Springhouse Branch Trail.

At 6 miles the trail arrives at the Jerry Flat backcountry campsite (#63, capacity 10), and at 7.2 miles the Upper Ripshin backcountry campsite (#62, capacity 12). The trail continues upstream alongside Noland Creek until reaching the confluence of Sassafras Branch at 8.8 miles, where it leaves Noland Creek to ascend the Noland Divide.

The Bald Creek backcountry campsite (#61, capacity 12) is located 200 yards upstream from the confluence of Sassafras Branch near the junction of Bald Branch and Noland Creek. Upstream from the Bald Creek site, the main stream is accessible by an unmaintained path that closely follows the stream to its confluence with Salola Branch at 10 miles. Clingmans Creek flows into the main stream at 10.8 miles.

Bearpen Branch

SIZE: Small
FISHING PRESSURE: Light
FISHING QUALITY: Fair
ACCESS: Remote
USGS QUADS: Noland Creek, NC

Bearpen Branch is purely a rainbow trout fishery. Fishing pressure on this small stream is light, despite its proximity to the North Shore Road. There are several unnamed tributaries that sport a few trout. Anglers should note that the terrain surrounding this little stream is very rugged.

Access: The mouth of the branch is located 1.7 miles upstream from the Noland Creek Trail starting point; there are no streamside trails.

Mill Creek

SIZE: Small
FISHING PRESSURE: Light
FISHING QUALITY: Very good
ACCESS: Remote
USGS QUADS: Clingmans Dome, NC-TN; Silers Bald, NC-TN

Mill Creek is one of the most important streams flowing into Noland Creek. It enters the main stream in the lovely Salola Valley, which was a busy community before the park was established, and later the site of a ranger station.

The lower portion of the stream is dominated by rainbow trout, but the headwaters still contain a healthy population of speckle trout.

Springhouse Branch, a noteworthy tributary of Mill Creek, flows into the main stream a short distance upstream from the Mill Creek Horse Camp site. It passes through a virgin forest, and contains only rainbow trout.

Access: The Springhouse Branch Trail offers limited access to Mill Creek and Springhouse Branch. It begins near the mouth of Mill Creek, and travels alongside the stream. At .7 mile upstream the trail crosses Mill Creek, and from that point continues up the Springhouse Branch. At 1.2 miles the trail leaves the stream to ascend Forney Ridge.

Bald Branch, Salola Branch, and Clingmans Creek

SIZE: All are small
FISHING PRESSURE: Closed
FISHING QUALITY: Very good
ACCESS: Remote
USGS QUADS: Clingmans Dome, NC-TN

These were some of the most popular brook trout streams in the park. The ease of descending from Clingmans Dome has proved to be something less than a blessing. All three rivulets were closed to all fishing in 1975 to protect the brook trout stock.

Access: There are no maintained trails offering access to any of these streams. Bald Branch flows into the main stream 9 miles upstream from Fontana Lake, or 4.5 miles from the Clingmans Dome Road. Salola Branch flows into the main stream 10 miles upstream from Fontana Lake, or 3.5 miles from the Clingmans Dome Road. Clingmans Creek flows into the main stream 10.8 miles upstream from Fontana Lake, or 2.7 miles from the Clingmans Dome Road.

Chapter 23

Forney Creek System

Forney Creek

SIZE: Medium
FISHING PRESSURE: Moderate to light
FISHING QUALITY: Very good
ACCESS: Fontana Lake; Forney Creek Trail
USGS QUADS: Noland Creek, NC; Silers Bald, NC-TN

Contrary to rumors that have circulated in the national sporting press in recent years, Forney Creek is not the weak sister of Hazel Creek. In fact, some local anglers like it better than Hazel Creek, which currently gets considerable fishing pressure.

Forney Creek is well-known to anyone who has spent time fishing in the Smokies, although it has not received the attention given several of the more highly-publicized fishing spots. Its remote location, plus its proximity to two of the most famous streams in the park—Hazel Creek and Deep Creek—spare it from the burden of excessive angling pressure. Local anglers from Tennessee and North Carolina are often about the only folks you will encounter fishing this sparkling stream.

The Forney Creek watershed was one of the most thoroughly devastated valleys in the Great Smoky Mountains National Park. It was the site of an intensive logging operation that clear-cut the coves and slopes without mercy. A massive forest fire that occurred during the mid-1920s, fed by the slash left behind by the loggers, consumed what remained of the valley's flora. As with many of the clear-cut sections of the Smokies, this one has slowly regrown under the protective sanctions of the National Park Service, yet deep scars heal slowly. Hikers and fishermen should not depend on old maps of this valley, since the devastation of the past altered many of the old trails.

*In recent seasons angling pressure at Forney
Creek has peaked, and for good reason*

Forney Creek possesses an exceptional population of frisky, colorful rainbow trout. Each summer a number of trophy-size 'bows are taken from this stream, although the majority of the fish fall into the 7- to 10-inch range. (The Forney Creek outlet bay on Fontana Lake offers very good fishing for winter run spawning rainbows.)

The lower reaches of this stream offer great fishing.

Brook trout can still be found in the stream's upper reaches. They are a fragile remnant population that under no circumstances should be disturbed. Habitat destruction dating back to the logging era and competition with rainbow trout have placed the future of the brookie in this watershed in grave danger.

The lower reaches of Forney Creek are silly with 2- to 4-pound smallmouth bass, and rock bass up to 1 pound. These fish are most commonly caught from the stream from June through September.

Forney Creek is located in the southeastern section of the Smokies. It is bound by Forney Ridge, Stateline Ridge, and Welch Ridge, and empties into Fontana Lake. Forney Creek has a well-developed network of tributaries, including Bear Creek, Advalorem Branch, Bee Gum Branch, Slap Camp Branch, Whitemans Glory Creek, Jonas Creek, Hugging Creek, Little Steeltrap Creek, and Steeltrap Creek

Access: There is no auto access to this stream; you reach it via boat, foot travel, or horseback. It is popular to visit this watershed by horseback, which allows for fast travel and ease in carrying gear. Several of the backcountry campsites along Forney Creek accommodate horseback travelers.

Upstream from Fontana Lake, you'll find the Forney Creek Trail, which begins at the mouth of the stream. Located approximately 100 yards upstream is the Lower Forney backcountry campsite (#74, capacity 12), an excellent fishing camp. At .6 mile upstream the trail arrives at the junction of Bear Branch and the trailhead of the Jumpup Trail. The Bear Creek backcountry campsite (#73, capacity 15) lies west of the stream junction.

The junction of Forney Creek and Bee Gum Branch is located upstream 2.6 miles. This is also the location of the trailhead for the Bee Gum Branch Trail, and nearby is the CCC Camp backcountry campsite (#71, capacity 12). At 3.3 miles the trail arrives at the junction of Slab Camp Branch, and at 4.1 miles is the junction of Jonas Creek. This is also the location of the trailhead of the Jonas Creek Trail and the Jonas Creek backcountry campsite (#70, capacity 12).

Huggins Creek flows into the main stream 5.3 miles upstream. The Huggins backcountry campsite (#69, capacity 12), also referred to as the Monteith campsite, is located near the stream's fork. The Forney Creek Trail passes a sign 6.9 miles up which indicates the direction of the Steeltrap backcountry campsite (#68, capacity 8). The trail crosses Little Steeltrap Creek at 7 miles, leaving the main stream of Forney Creek to travel along the gentle slopes of Wild Cherry Ridge. Near 8.8 miles the trail fords Steeltrap Creek and resumes its streamside ascent of the ridge alongside Forney Creek. The trail continues to furnish excellent access to Forney Creek to about the 9.7-mile mark, where it then leaves Forney Creek for the last time, to later terminate 1 mile from Clingmans Dome.

Bear Branch

SIZE: Small
FISHING PRESSURE: Light
FISHING QUALITY: Fair
ACCESS: Remote
USGS QUADS: Noland Creek, NC

Bear Branch is a small stream that offers fair fishing for stream-bound rainbow trout. It cannot be said this is the finest stream in the Forney Creek watershed. Most of the rainbow trout taken in this stream are below creel size (averaging 5 to 7 inches in length).

Access: Bear Branch is accessible upstream from its confluence with Forney Creek via the Jumpup Ridge Trail. The trailhead is located at the mouth of Bear Branch .6 mile upstream from Fontana Lake. It provides intermittent access to the stream for 2 miles. The trail reaches Poplar Flats at 2.8 miles, and leaves the stream at that point.

Bee Gum Branch

SIZE: Small
FISHING PRESSURE: Light
FISHING QUALITY: Fairly good
ACCESS: Remote
USGS QUADS: Noland Creek, NC

Bee Gum Branch is a decent little trout stream. There are a fair number of cascades and pools holding rainbow trout. The stream is heavily overgrown with laurel and rhododendron, making fishing difficult.

Access: Bee Gum Branch flows into the main stream 2.8 miles upstream from Fontana Lake. Fair access to the stream is provided by the Bee Gum Branch Trail. For the first 2.3 miles, the stream is often several hundred yards from the trail. At 2.8 miles, the trail leaves the stream to ascend Forney Ridge.

Jonas Creek

SIZE: Small
FISHING PRESSURE: Light
FISHING QUALITY: Very good
ACCESS: Remote
USGS QUADS: Silers Bald, NC-TN

Jonas Creek is a dandy little trout stream. Numerous deep holes harbor some fine rainbows. You will probably have the entire stream to yourself any time you decide to wet a line there. As an added dividend, there are several tributaries in this little valley that are very worthwhile to fish. Adventurous anglers can find side streams working alive with trout that seldom see more than a dozen bronzed hooks per year. Two feeder streams of merit are Scarlett Ridge Creek and Little Jonas Creek.

Access: The Jonas Creek Trail provides access to the stream. The trailhead is located 4.1 miles upstream from Fontana Lake near the mouth of Jonas Creek. At 1.3 miles, the trail forsakes the main stream and continues upstream alongside Little Jonas Creek, then at 1.7 miles it crosses Yanu Branch, leaving Little Jonas Creek. The trail then makes a series of switchbacks until 2.7 miles, where it comes within 50 feet of Yanu Branch, before leaving to ascend Welch Ridge.

Huggins Creek

SIZE: Small
FISHING PRESSURE: Closed
FISHING QUALITY: Very good
ACCESS: Remote
USGS QUADS: Silers Bald, NC-TN

Huggins Creek is an excellent example of the plight of the southern Appalachian brook trout. As late as 1975, fish and wildlife surveys showed populations of brook trout in both Huggins Creek and Little Huggins Creek, but present data do not support the presence of brookies in this streamshed.

The four prongs to Huggins Creek begin at an altitude of more than 4,800 feet. However, even with such a tributary system, it appears the ever-encroaching rainbows have perhaps won out.

Access: Huggins Creek flows between Suli Ridge and Loggy Ridge. There is an unmaintained trail that begins near the mouth of the stream, and follows alongside to the headwaters.

Chapter 24

Hazel Creek System

Hazel Creek

SIZE: Large
FISHING PRESSURE: Moderate to very heavy in the lower
portion; relatively light to modern in the upper portion
above 2,500 feet
FISHING QUALITY: Excellent
ACCESS: Fontana Lake; Hazel Creek Trail
USGS QUADS: Tuskeegee, NC; Thunderhead, NC-TN; Silers Bald,
NC-TN

Hazel Creek has been termed the crown jewel of trout fishing
in the Great Smoky Mountains National Park, and touted by most
major outdoor publications in past years. Hazel Creek has all the
needed qualifications to claim being the finest freestone stream in
the southern Appalachian Mountains. One of the secrets of this
stream's excellent fishing is the abundant insect life. Caddis flies
dominate, although you will find that prolific hatches of
Stenonema mayflies get the attention of trout during the summer.
The lower portion, dominated by rainbow and brown trout, is
highly productive for large terrestrial imitations such as the
grasshopper and jassid. Here, the stream rushes past old homesteads and fragrant orchards, forming many long, slow pools, perfect for floating a cinnamon ant pattern. I feel nothing will put the
adrenaline in your system faster than a lightning-fast strike from a
trout coaxed from one of these beautiful pools.

Brookies can be found in the main stream beyond an elevation
of 3,040 feet, one of the lowest elevations for brookies in a major
streamshed in the Smokies. Hazel Creek has one of the loftiest
tributary systems in the park. These headwater streams provide
some of the finest brook trout habitat in the Smokies.

The upper reaches of Hazel Creek harbor big brookies.

The lower reaches of Hazel Creek not only hold trout, but healthy populations of largemouth, smallmouth, and rock bass. This is one of the very few places in the Great Smoky Mountains National Park where largemouth bass can be caught by fly-fishermen.

Hazel Creek is located in the southeast section of the Smokies. It is bound by Welch Ridge and Jenkins Ridge. Its headwaters are located beneath the slopes of Stateline Ridge, and from there the stream flows into Fontana Lake. Primary tributaries of Hazel Creek are Sugar Fork, Bone Valley Creek, Walker Creek, and Proctor Creek.

The Hazel Creek watershed was one of the most heavily devastated in the Smokies. The Ritter Logging Company removed virtually every stand of virgin timber from the valley, in an operation that took nearly twenty years. The loggers laid rail lines almost 13 miles up Hazel Creek to enable them to haul the fallen giants to the sawmills. Proctor was a booming sawmill town of more then one thousand people, and the center of the valley's life.

Upon receiving stewardship of the Smokies, the National Park Service found many residents reluctant to abandon their mountain homesteads. Even today, you may encounter groups of mountain folk on the trail, carrying floral arrangements to be placed on the graves of loved ones buried in the park, an annual event for the people who still feel a part of these mountains of their birth.

The forest has regrown nicely under the protection of the National Park Service. The area has an abundance of plant life and, not too surprisingly, many varieties of domestic plants. Hazel Creek can boast of one of the park's few beaver colonies. There are no beaver dams on the stream, but the busy beaver have downed a large number of trees alongside the stream, which provide badly-needed cover for trout.

Access: All roads leading into Hazel Creek were closed during World War II when Fontana Lake was impounded. The isolation has helped spare the stream, and enabled it to maintain high-quality fishing.

Crossing the lake by boat is perhaps the easiest and most popular way to visit Hazel Creek. For a modest sum, the operators of the Fontana Village Resort Marina provide transportation across the lake by arrangement. One really nice feature of going this route is being relieved of worrying about the safety of your boat.

You may encounter a variety of strange-looking vehicles on these trails that appear to be a cross between a wheelbarrow and a bicycle. These versatile contraptions, known as "Smoky Mountain pushcarts," are constructed of lightweight materials such as tubular aluminum and tires from ten-speed bicycles. Such backcountry rarities as coolers full of perishable foods, lanterns, cots, and big tents are transported up the stream in these rigs by local fishermen unwilling to compromise their fishing trips with the usual backcountry fare of freeze-dried foods and cramped hiking tents.

The Hazel Creek Trail follows the stream. The trailhead is located near the mouth of the stream on Fontana Lake. The Proctor backcountry campsite (#86, capacity 20), located .5 mile upstream from the lake, is a popular base camp. Upstream from this site is the "Horseshoe," noted for its excellent trout fishing.

At 3.3 miles is the Sawdust Pile backcountry campsite (#85, capacity 20), also popular with backcountry fishermen. The poetic "Brown Pool" is nearby. Its famous waters have been the sight of the day's last cast for countless anglers.

At 5 miles the trail reaches the junction of Sugar Fork and the trailhead of the Sugar Fork Trail. Located nearby is the Sugar Fork backcountry campsite (#84, capacity 8), which is well-suited as a fishing camp. At 5.6 miles the trail arrives at the mouth of Bone Valley Creek, also the trailhead for the Bone Valley Trail and the site of the Bone Valley backcountry campsite (#83, capacity 20). At 8.6 miles the trail reaches the Calhoun Camp backcountry campsite (N.P.S. #82, capacity 15), and continues to the junction of Hazel Creek and Walker Creek at 9.5 mile. The junction of Proctor Creek and the Proctor Creek backcountry campsite (#81, capacity 15) is at 10.5 miles.

The trail upstream from the Proctor Creek site becomes steeper and more difficult to travel. At 13.5 miles the trail reaches the Hazel Creek Cascades backcountry campsite (#80, capacity 12). located at an elevation of more than 4,000 feet, well into the heart of the brook trout fishery. The trail upstream from the cascades is steep, though open and passable.

Sugar Fork

Size: Small
Fishing Pressure: Fairly light
Fishing Quality: Very good
Access: Hazel Creek Trail; Sugar Fork Trail
Usgs Quads: Tuskeegee, NC; Thunderhead, NC-TN

Big browns and smallmouth bass abound in the lower reaches of Hazel Creek.

Sugar Fork is the first significant feeder stream encountered up Hazel Creek. It is a nice little stream—although often overlooked by anglers—offering excellent rainbow trout fishing, with an abundance of cascades that provide interesting fishing almost any day of the year.

Haw Gap Branch and Little Sugar Fork are tributaries of angling merit.

Access: The Sugar Fork Trail starts 5 miles upstream from the lake. At .5 mile the Sugar Fork Trail reaches the mouth of Haw Gap Branch and the junction of Haw Gap Trail. The Haw Gap Trail offers access to the branch. At 1.7 miles the trail arrives at the junction of Little Sugar Fork. A short distance upstream from this point, the trail leaves the stream.

Bone Valley Creek

Size: Medium
Fishing Pressure: Moderately light
Fishing Quality: Excellent
Access: Bone Valley Trail
Usgs Quads: Tuskeegee, NC; Thunderhead, NC-TN

Anyone taking the time to visit the Hazel Creek area should spend at least one day exploring and fishing Bone Valley. Bone Valley came by its name in the late 1880s, when an unexpected and severe late-spring blizzard hit the area. Cattle, already brought up from the valley, were caught in the midst of the storm's fury. In their efforts to stay warm, the cattle huddled together, one on top of the other. Their efforts failed, and huge stacks of bones were left to bleach in the summer sun. Henceforth, the area was known as Bone Valley.

Bone Valley Creek enters the main stream 5.6 miles upstream from the lake, and offers excellent rainbow and brook trout fishing. It is a good-size stream with a challenging mixture of riffles and pools.

Noteworthy tributaries of Bone Valley Creek include Wooly Branch, a good little trout stream, although very overgrown; Defeat Branch, a personal favorite, sporting both rainbow and brook trout; Desolation Branch, a brook trout stream; and Roaring Fork, a popular brookie stream.

Access: The Bone Valley Trail begins at the mouth of the stream, 5.6 miles upstream from Fontana Lake. The trail follows alongside the stream, and reaches the Hall Cabin at 1.7 miles at the end of the maintained portion of the trail, where an unmaintained path continues upstream. At the mouth of Desolation Branch the trail then begins following alongside the small tributary.

Walker Creek

SIZE: Small
FISHING PRESSURE: Light
FISHING QUALITY: Excellent
ACCESS: Unnamed path
USGS QUADS: Thunderhead, NC-TN

Walker Creek is a small, often overlooked trout stream of very good fishing quality. The trout here are of average size, but are not nearly as leader shy as the fish in the main stream. There are rainbow trout in the lower section of the stream, but above the falls the stream is all speckle trout.

Access: The stream's mouth is 9.5 miles up stream from Fontana Lake. The stream is only accessible via an unmaintained path that begins at the mouth of the stream and follows alongside to its headwaters.

Proctor Creek

SIZE: Small
FISHING PRESSURE: Light
FISHING QUALITY: Excellent
ACCESS: Unnamed path
USGS QUADS: Thunderhead, NC-TN

Proctor Creek offers anglers a chance to fish in a stream abounding with lively trout amidst an exceptionally beautiful forest setting. This is a popular trout stream, and barbless hooks are definitely in order for all sportsmen.

Proctor Creek flows into the main stream 10.5 miles upstream from the lake. This stream has a well-developed tributary system. Long Cove Creek and James Camp Branch are favorites among anglers.

Access: The stream's mouth is 10.5 miles upstream from Fontana Lake. There is an excellent unmaintained path that follows alongside the stream to its headwaters.

Chapter 25

Eagle Creek System

Eagle Creek

SIZE: Medium
FISHING PRESSURE: Moderately light to heavy
FISHING QUALITY: Very good, particularly upstream from
Pinnacle Creek
ACCESS: Fontana Lake; Eagel Creek Trail
USGS QUADS: Fontana Dam, NC; Thunderhead, NC-TN; Cades
Cove, NC-TN

When my first trout fishing guide to these streams was published, Eagle Creek was one of the most overlooked waters in the
national park. That has changed significantly over the last fifteen
years. Fishing pressure is up, but the quality of fishing in these
waters remains high.

Eagle Creek is nestled in a secluded valley in the southwest
corner of the Great Smoky Mountains National Park. Its remote
location has spared the stream's trout the daily ritual of scanning
every morsel for a hidden hook. It receives only a moderate
amount of angling pressure, and there are few signs of overuse
anywhere in this area. The backcountry campsites are clean and
untrampled.

Brook trout still have a few good strongholds in the Eagle Creek
watershed, notably Gunna Creek and Asgini Branch. This watershed was not as heavily logged as the nearby Hazel Creek Valley,
thus the flow was not defiled by such lethal logging byproducts as
silt and tannic acid (from the decomposing tree bark and slash).
Although it is only a matter of conjecture, many knowledgeable
anglers feel the strong presence of the rainbow trout in the stream
is partially responsible for the deterioration of the brook trout
fishery.

Often overlooked, Eagle Creek is a fine little trout stream.

In recent years, a few brown trout have immigrated into the main stream from Fontana Lake. Their presence is insignificant compared to that of the abundant rainbow trout, which have dominion over the main stream. Rainbow trout fishing is very good here.

The lower reaches of Eagle Creek sport a limited smallmouth and rock bass fishery. These fish are found upstream from the mouth of the stream for at least 3 miles.

This stream offers its share of surprises.

Eagle Creek is bound by Jenkins Ridge, Stateline Ridge, and Twenty Mile Ridge. It flows into Fontana Lake a short distance from the dam. Eagle Creek's tributaries of interest to fishermen are Lost Creek, Pinnacle Creek, Ekaneetlee Creek, Tub Mill Creek, and Gunnas Creek.

Access: No roads lead to the Eagle Creek watershed, as it was permanently sealed off during World War II by Fontana Lake's impoundment of the Little Tennessee River. Crossing the lake by boat is the most popular means of visiting Eagle Creek. Light boats equipped with small outboard motors or canoes can be rented from the operators of the Fontana Village Resort Marina. Additionally, the operators of the marina will be happy to make arrangements with fishermen to take them to the mouth of the stream and later pick them up. I have made use of this handy service on a number of occasions, and highly recommend it.

Anglers wishing to visit Eagle Creek, but preferring to keep both feet on solid ground, will discover that Lost Cove Trail offers the easiest access to Eagle Creek from an auto access standpoint. This route makes it necessary to begin on the Appalachian Trail crossing of Fontana Dam. Traveling north along the Appalachian Trail 3.7 miles to Sassafras Gap, the trail reaches the junction of the Lost Cove Trail. The Lost Cove Trail descends down the ridge to the right, and at 3 miles reaches the Lost Cove Creek backcountry campsite (#90, capacity 12), a lakeside camp near the mouth of Eagle Creek.

Upstream access is provided by the Eagle Creek Trail, which begins at the mouth of the stream, and follows alongside the creek. The trail rounds Horseshoe Bend at .5 mile and reaches the mouth of Pinnacle Creek at 1 mile, which is also the site of the trailhead for the Pinnacle Creek Trail. The Eagle Creek Trail continues upstream alongside the main stream to the confluence of Ekaneetlee Creek at 2 miles, where the Lower Ekaneetlee backcountry campsite (#89, capacity 8), a superb fishing camp, is located. Continuing upstream, the Eagle Creek Trail reaches the Eagle Creek Islands backcountry campsite (#99, capacity 10) at 3.5 miles, then continues its upstream climb and at 5 miles reaches the confluence of Tub Mill Creek and Gunna Creek. This is the beginning point of Eagle Creek proper. The Big Walnut backcountry campsite (#97, capacity 10), the last camping spot along the trail, is located here. The Eagle Creek Trail continues upstream alongside Gunna Creek (see Gunna Creek).

Pinnacle Creek

SIZE: Small
FISHING PRESSURE: Light
FISHING QUALITY: Fair
ACCESS: Remote; Pinnacle Creek Trail
USGS QUADS: Fontana Dam, NC; Thunderhead, NC-TN

Pinnacle Creek is probably the most overlooked feeder stream in the Eagle Creek system. It holds a few good rainbow trout, and there is a nice campsite upstream that makes a fine, secluded fishing base.

Access: The Pinnacle Creek Trail provides good access to the stream. It begins at the mouth of Pinnacle Creek, and follows alongside the stream. At 1.5 miles the trail arrives at the Pinnacle backcountry campsite (#88, capacity 8). The trail continues along the stream for 2.8 miles, where it leaves the stream and ascends to Pickens Gap.

Ekaneetlee Creek

SIZE: Small
FISHING PRESSURE: Light
FISHING QUALITY: Excellent
ACCESS: Remote
USGS QUADS: Fontana Dam, NC; Cades Cove, NC-TN

Ekaneetlee Creek is a fine little trout stream that flows alongside an ancient Indian pathway. There is a good population of speckle trout above the 2,900-foot mark, with rainbows filling the gap between the main stream and that point.

Big Tommy Branch and Adams Hollow Branch, tributaries of Ekaneetlee Creek, are a sure bet for a day of good fishing.

Access: The Ekaneetlee Manway provides very good access to the stream. Ekaneetlee Creek flows into Eagle Creek 2 miles upstream from Fontana Lake. The trail begins at the mouth of the stream, and follows alongside to its headwaters, before ascending to

Ekaneetlee Gap. Note: This is an unmaintained trail that is usually kept open by fishermen; however, inexperienced backcountry travelers should exercise caution if they decide to visit here.

Tub Mill Creek

SIZE: Small
FISHING PRESSURE: Light
FISHING QUALITY: Very good
ACCESS: Remote
USGS QUADS: Cades Cove, NC-TN

Tub Mill Creek flows together with Gunna Creek to form Eagle Creek. It has a well-developed tributary network that sports both rainbow and brook trout.

Asgini Branch and Lawson Gant Lot Branch, tributaries of Tub Mill Creek, offer good fishing.

Access: Tub Mill Creek flows into the main stream 5 miles upstream from Fontana Lake. The stream is reached at this point from the Eagle Creek Trail. No maintained trails lend access upstream from the mouth of the stream.

Gunna Creek

SIZE: Small
FISHING PRESSURE: Light
FISHING QUALITY: Excellent
ACCESS: Remote; Eagle Creek Trail
USGS QUADS: Cades Cove, NC-TN; Thunderhead, NC-TN

Gunna Creek is the upstream extension of the main portion of Eagle Creek. It holds a mixed population of rainbow and brook trout. Its extreme headwaters were closed to all fishing in 1975 to protect the brook trout, which prosper there. Massive hemlocks grown alongside the stream, many covered with cool, green growths of thick moss that help make this a delightful place to fish.

Paw Paw Creek and Spence Cabin Branch, tributaries of Gunna Creek, hold populations of colorful speckle trout.

Access: The Eagle Creek Trail follows alongside Gunna Creek upstream from its confluence with Tub Mill Creek. The trail passes by the mouth of Paw Paw Creek at 6 miles (upstream from Fontana Lake), then follows alongside this lovely mountain brook 8 miles before leaving, to later terminate on the ridge at the Appalachian Trail.

Chapter 26

Twenty Mile Creek System

Twenty Mile Creek

SIZE: Medium
FISHING PRESSURE: Moderately light
FISHING QUALITY: Good all season
ACCESS: Twenty Mile Creek Trail
USGS QUADS: Tapoco, NC; Fontana, NC

Twenty Mile Creek is one of the least-known streams in the park. Local anglers have long considered this their secret preserve. The stream is located in the extreme southern portion of the Smokies, isolated from almost all commercial development. Visiting anglers should take the time to discover this gem. Twenty Mile Creek is a productive stream, sporting a scrappy population of rainbow trout in its fast flow. The stream has a nice distribution of deep pools, pocket water, and shallow runs. It is sometimes a challenge to fish, but a well-placed cast will bring rewards.

Twenty Mile Creek is a rainbow trout fishery, although a rare brown trout, up from Cheoah Lake, will occasionally be taken in the downstream section. Brook trout are as rare here as chicken teeth.

Twenty Mile Creek is bound by Wolfe Ridge, Greer Knob, and Twenty Mile Ridge, and flows into Cheoah Lake. It is of medium size, with a small tributary system. Moore Spring Branch and Dalton Branch offer the best feeder stream fishing in this watershed.

Access: The Twenty Mile Creek Ranger Station is located 2.8 miles east of the US 129/NC 28 junction. Drive past the ranger station to the parking area, where the Twenty Mile Creek Trail begins. At .6 mile the trail reaches the mouth of Moore Spring Branch and the junction of the Wolfe Ridge Trail.

The Wolfe Ridge Trail follows Moore Spring Branch, and at 4 miles arrives at the Wolfe Ridge backcountry campsite (#95, capacity 8). The mouth of Dalton Branch is near this campsite.

The Twenty Mile Creek Trail continues along Twenty Mile Creek, and at 1.8 miles arrives at the Twenty Mile backcountry campsite (#93, capacity 14). At 4.5 miles the trail leaves the stream for the last time to ascend to Shuckstack Fire Tower.

Chapter 27

Abrams Creek System

Abrams Creek

SIZE: At the mouth, the stream is large; in the Cades Cove area it is medium

FISHING PRESSURE: Moderate to very heavy

FISHING QUALITY: Excellent

ACCESS: TN 72; Happy Valley Road; Rabbit Creek Trail, Cooper Road Trail, Abrams Falls trail, Anthony Creek trail

USGS QUADS: Cades Cove, NC-TN; Thunderhead, NC-TN; Calderwood, NC-TN; Blockhouse, TN

REGULATIONS: From Mill Creek junction downstream to the embayment waters, Abrams Creek is designated Experimental Fish Management Water, and may be fished according to general regulations, except the size limit is 12 inches or longer

Of all the streams in the Great Smoky Mountains National Park, this is my favorite. I have spent many memorable hours on this fine stream, and look forward to many more. Abrams Creek is not only the finest rainbow trout stream in the park, but also the most interesting and unique.

Stream surveys conducted by fishery biologist Steve Moore of the National Park Service confirmed what this writer and many other anglers have long known: this is the most trout-rich water in the national park. The scientific stream survey revealed Abrams Creek has twice has many pounds of trout per surface acre as any other stream in the Smokies. One of the most popular fishing destinations in the Great Smokies, angling pressure on this stream has gone up significantly over the last fifteen years.

Abrams Creek also is the top smallmouth and rock bass fishery in the national park. Smallies up to 7 pounds are regularly caught from this stream.

The spring caddis fly hatches here are equal to any found in the southern Appalachian Mountains. Abrams Creek can also boast one of the Smokie's most spectacular hatches of Quadwing yellow mayflies. It is not only the fly-fishermen who find this stream an inviting haven. The stream is literally working alive with forage fish, whose food value to the trout affords the spinner fisherman excellent opportunities.

Abrams Creek is one of many streams in the park still known by its Indian name. Old Abram was the chief of the Cherokee village of Chilhowee, which was located at the mouth of Abrams Creek on the Little Tennessee River. He met an untimely and gruesome death at the hands of a vengeful 17-year-old lad named John Kirk. Old Abram and four other Cherokee chiefs from the neighboring Citico area were being held prisoner, as they were thought responsible for the deaths of Kirk's mother and ten brothers and sisters. Kirk entered the lodge where the five chiefs were being held, and killed all five with blows from an ax. It was later proved that Creek Indians, not Cherokees, were responsible for the Kirk family massacre. General John Sevier ordered Kirk to be hanged for the murder of the innocent Cherokee leaders, but the flamboyant militiaman then refused to allow the execution to be carried out, and subsequently, Kirk was released. John Sevier went on to become the governor of Tennessee, and my great-great-great-great-grandfather, John Kirk, resettled much farther north in Nolichucky Valley.

Abrams Creek's headwaters begin on the slopes beneath the grassy balds of Spense Field and Russell Field. The stream from that point flows into Chilhowee Reservoir. The Abrams Creek watershed is located in the southwest section of the Smokies. Its principal tributaries are Panther, Rabbit, and Mill creeks. Abrams Creek is basically a rainbow/brown trout fishery. Brook trout have almost vanished from this watershed.

The mouth of Abrams Creek is actually part of the Chilhowee Reservoir impoundment. The first couple of miles upstream from the lake offer only mediocre trout fishing. This section of the stream is often difficult to travel, due to the impoundment and the dense flora around the stream.

It is a common sight in the winter season to view boats full of warmly-clad anglers anchored at the mouth of Abrams Creek in the Chilhowee Reservoir. These knowledgeable fishermen brave the sometimes severe winter weather for a chance at the angling bounty of the rainbow trout spawning run. Winter rains spark the instinctive mating drive of these trout, commonly weighing 3 to 8 pounds, which spend the majority of their lives in the cool depths of the TVA impoundment, waxing fat on forage fish. Before swimming upstream, these hefty milt- and roe-laden trout often spend a day or two at the mouth of the stream, waiting for precisely the right moment before embarking on their quest. It is during this quasi-immobile period at the mouth of the stream that fishermen often score limits of trout of a much greater size than is generally possible during other times of the year. The stream and Chilhowee Reservoir are open to fishing year-round. Anchoring a boat at the mouth of the stream is both legal and profitable.

Abrams Creek at the Abrams Creek Campground offers excellent trout fishing. The stream has many long, green pools, commonly stretching over 300 feet. Here a large number of downed trees litter the stream bank, providing shelter for many wise, old, mossy-back trout. This section of the stream is a favorite haunt of several of the fine local East Tennessee trout fishermen. It is seldom crowded, making this a good bet for a day of solitary fishing.

Upstream from the campground lies an area known as Little Bottoms. This is a somewhat remote section of the stream that offers superior trout fishing for those willing to make the two-mile walk. At Abrams Falls the stream plunges 25 feet into a deep emerald pool. The falls' pool harbors many of the stream's largest trout, and the pool's size allows fly-fishermen plenty of backcasting room. Unfortunately for anglers, swimmers and sightseers also find Abrams Falls much to their liking. Early morning and late evenings are usually the only times anglers can find relative peace on this lovely pool.

Abrams Creek upstream from the falls to Cades Cove is Smoky Mountains trout fishing at its finest. The stream forms a small loop above the falls that is seven-tenths of a mile long, and requires nearly half a day to properly fish. Immediately upstream, a second loop known as the Horseshoe rounds Arbustus Ridge. The Horseshoe is one mile long, and it is advisable to allow a whole day to fish this sometimes tricky stretch of creek. Both the falls loop and the Horseshoe offer superb trout fishing. The stream is subject to heavy fishing pressure from both sportsmen and poachers. Despite this, rainbow trout in the 3- to 4-pound class abound. During May, when several species of caddis fly larvae enter the pupae stage and begin darting about beneath the surface, the section of the creek literally comes alive with feeding action.

During the spring and winter months, the cove section provides good rainbow trout and excellent, if difficult, brown trout opportunities. This area is very overgrown, and thoroughly entangled with submerged root structure.

Abrams Creek is better known as Anthony Creek upstream from the Cades Cove Historic Area. Anthony Creek abounds with creel-size rainbow trout. The dense laurel overgrowths surrounding the stream make taking one of these bejeweled little fish a soul-satisfying feat any angler can appreciate. Anthony Creek forks .5 mile upstream from Cades Cove. The Left Prong originates on the northern slopes of Ledbetter Ridge, and the Right Prong flows off the slopes of Spense Field. Both prongs of Anthony Creek offer delightful trout fishing amidst a primeval hemlock forest setting.

One of the most unique aspects of Abrams Creek is the metamorphosis the stream undergoes while traversing the Cades Cove Historic Area. Cades Cove sits atop a huge limestone bed. As the creek enters the cove, over 60 percent of the stream filters underground and makes a subsurface passage through the limestone before rejoining the stream near the Abrams Falls parking area. This subsurface trek dramatically increases the stream's generally acidic composition of a pH of 6 to 6.7, to a mild pH of 7.1 to 8.3. The remaining surface-flowing portion of Abrams Creek weaves its way through the cove's pasture fields, where approximately five hundred head of cattle are grazed. Here the stream receives nutrients from the cattle's waste, which rain washes into the stream. These added twists to the stream's composition bring both blessings and problems.

The fecal bacteria from the cattle manure make the water downstream from the cove unfit for human use. The near constant presence of the cattle alongside the stream accelerates an already touchy siltation problem. Many gravel spawning beds have been rendered useless by siltation. The silt settles on virtually every rock in the stream, making them as hazardous as ice on a winter's day. Wading Abrams Creek is a dangerous adventure for even the most experienced and daring trout fisherman.

The benefits from the twofold change Abrams Creek is forced to cope with seem to outweigh the problems, at least from the angler's point of view. The added nutrients and the richness gained from the limestone create an ideal habitat for many aquatic invertebrates, particularly the Trichoptera (caddis flies). This radical concentration of macroinvertebrates supports a staggering number of rough, forage, and game fish, especially in the first 4 miles of flow. The obvious reason for this is the exaggerated nutrient base found in this unique stream. Of all the streams in the Smoky Mountains National Park, only Hazel Creek can rival this stream as an angler's paradise.

Access: Road Access: The Abrams Creek watershed is accessible by automobile from several points. Where the stream flows into Chilhoee Reservoir, it is easily reached from TN 72. Access is also available from Abrams Creek Campground, which is located 7 miles north of US 129 on the Happy Valley Road.

At Cades Cove there are two primary points of access to the stream. The Abrams Falls parking area allows access to the stream as it leaves the cove. Access to Anthony Creek can be made from the Cades Cove picnic area. The Cades Cove Loop Road is no longer opened early every morning. It remains closed until noon on Saturdays.

Trail Access: At the park boundary, near the mouth of Abrams Creek, there is an old, unmaintained trail that roughly follows the ascent of the stream. This is the only path to the downstream area. This seldom-traveled trail is often difficult to locate, and is not recommended for inexperienced hikers. At some points the trail is 700 feet from the stream. At the confluence of Bell Branch, 4 miles upstream from TN 72, the path receives much greater amounts of foot travel. The trail from that point weaves alongside Abrams Creek for 2.8 miles to the Rabbit Creek Trail junction.

From the junction point, the Rabbit Creek Trail becomes the stream's access trail for anglers. It follows the stream to the Abrams Creek Campground. This facility offers primitive campsite accommodations, and is easily reached by auto.

Upstream from the campground, the stream is reached by hiking north on the Cooper Road Trail. This trail leaves the stream .6 mile upstream from the campground. At 1 mile the Cooper Road Trail intersects the Little Bottoms Manway. Located at the trail junction is a spacious backcountry campsite known as Little Bottoms (#17, capacity 10). The Little Bottoms Manway follows the stream up to Abrams Falls Trail. The Falls Trail follows the upstream progress of the stream 2.5 miles to the falls parking area. There is no trail access to Abrams Creek as it passes through the Cades Cove Historic Area.

Anthony Creek, as Abrams Creek is known prior to entering the cove, is accessible from the Anthony Creek Trail. This trail begins at the Cades Cove picnic area. The trail runs adjacent to the stream until the stream forks at 1.5 miles. The Anthony Creek Trail follows the Right Prong of Anthony Creek 2.8 miles before leaving the stream to climb the southern slopes of Cold Water Knob. Located 2.5 miles upstream on the Anthony Creek Trail is the Anthony Creek backcountry campsite (#9, capacity 6).

The Russell Field Trail follows the Left Prong of Anthony Creek upstream 1 mile, then veers right, leaving the stream to ascend Ledbetter Ridge.

Panther Creek

SIZE: Medium to small
FISHING PRESSURE: Light to moderate
FISHING QUALITY: Excellent
ACCESS: Parsons Branch Road
USGS QUADS: Calderwood, NC-TN
REGULATIONS: This stream is part of the Experimental Fish Management Water, and may be fished according to general regulations, except the size limit is 12 inches or longer

Panther Creek is the first significant tributary encountered upstream from the mouth of Abrams Creek. This is an excellent trout stream, holding a large population of rainbow trout. Although only a fair-size stream, Panther Creek offers a wide variety of stream conditions that can tax even a hardened Appalachian trouter. The downstream portion of the creek receives only a moderate amount of fishing pressure, while upstream near the headwaters angling pressure is more intense.

Panther Creek begins its seaward journey beneath the southern slopes of High Point. Bear Den Branch, a tributary of Panther Creek, is worthy of mention to trout fishermen. It flows off the slopes of Pole Cat Ridge, and literally swarms with fat little rainbow trout that seldom see a feathered hook dangling from a willowy fly rod.

Access: Panther Creek is accessible by auto from Parsons Branch Road. This road begins in Cades Cove, off the Loop Road, and crosses Panther Creek at 3.5 miles, at an elevation of 2,540 feet. From this point, anglers are free to fish either upstream or downstream.

The mouth of Panther Creek is reached via an old, unmaintained trail, which is a spur trail from the path that connects the Abrams Creek Campground with TN 72. Panther Creek Manway leaves the Abrams Creek Trail at the first stream crossing, and for a short distance follows the downstream progress of Abrams Creek. Hikers must then negotiate a hazardous crossing of Abrams Creek at the mouth of Panther Creek. It is often advisable to make this crossing in a rubber raft or canoe. On the other side of the stream, the trail then closely follows the stream for 4 miles before leaving the stream to ascend the southern slopes of Bunker Hill. Bear Den Branch flows into the main stream four-tenths of a mile upstream from the trail's last contact with the stream. There is no additional access to the stream until Parsons Branch Road makes contact with the stream at 2,540 feet.

The Hannah Mountain Trail briefly follows along two small tributaries of Panther Creek; however, neither of these small brooks have angling merit. There are no backcountry campsites in the Panther Creek system.

Rabbit Creek

SIZE: Fairly small
FISHING PRESSURE: Light
FISHING QUALITY: Good
ACCESS: Parsons Branch Road; Rabbit Creek Trail
USGS QUADS: Calderwood, NC-TN
REGULATIONS: Part of the Experimental Fish Management Water, and may be fished according to general regulations, except the size limit is 12 inches or longer

Rabbit Creek is one of those nifty little streams trout fishermen become notoriously sullen about when other anglers query them for its secrets. I have never encountered another angler, or even evidence of their presence, along this rivulet. Rabbit Creek enters Abrams Creek 3.5 miles upstream from the Abrams Creek Campground. Rabbit Creek's icy waters flow from springs located on the sides of Hannah Mountain. Rainbow trout are the dominant species to be found in this stream. There are numerous small tributaries, but none begin at over 2,800 feet. Nearly all of these tiny brooks are inhabited by trout.

Access: Rabbit Creek is accessible from Parsons Branch Road. This road begins in Cades Cove and runs alongside the stream for over 1 mile. The stream is reached by foot travel from the Rabbit Creek Trail. This trail begins at the Abrams Falls parking area in Cades Cove. The trail reaches the stream at 4.7 miles. At this stream crossing is the popular Rabbit Creek backcountry campsite (#15, capacity 8). This is the only contact with the stream for this trail.

Mill Creek

SIZE: Small
FISHING PRESSURE: Moderate
FISHING QUALITY: Fair
ACCESS: Cades Cove Loop Road
USGS QUADS: Cades Cove, TN

Mill Creek flows into Abrams Creek at the Abrams Falls parking area. It is most interesting to stand at the junction of these nearly equal-in-size streams, and observe the intermingling of their dramatically different waters. Abrams Creek, prior to joining Mill Creek, is a milky, limestone rich stream. Its bottom is sandy bedrock. Mill Creek, in sharp contrast, is a crystal-clear, acidic, boulder-strewn rivulet typical of most streams in the Smokies. At the confluence, you can easily observe a marked difference in the streams. To the right, the tinted water of Abrams Creek flows on, holding stubbornly to its former character. To the left, Mill Creek's rusty bottom and clear water fight the inevitable clouding. Only after flowing several hundred feet downstream do the two water types intermingle to make their identity indistinguishable.

Mill Creek is a challenging stream of fair fishing quality. Many of the larger fish instinctively move downstream to Abrams Creek, where food is more abundant. Mill Creek is an easy stream to get around on, and as an added bonus receives only moderate angling pressure. In early spring, a short jaunt up this creek with a good stonefly nymph imitation will make you a firm disciple of small-stream trouting. I highly recommend Mill Creek and its tributaries to those wishing a short, easy fishing trip in the Great Smoky Mountains National Park.

Mill Creek's tributaries flow off McCampbell and Forge knobs. Mill Creek forks behind the Becky Cable House in Cades Cove. The right prong is known as Forge Creek, and the left prong is Mill Creek. Forge Creek is also worthy of angling merit. This rocky little branch offers fine fishing to those fishermen deft enough to drop a small fly beneath its many foaming cascades. Ekaneetlee Branch, a tributary of Forge Creek, holds a population of rainbow trout. This is a very small creek, but one with a good sprinkling of cascade pools of surprising depth. It is a good stream to depend on for a meal of fresh trout if you plan a backcountry trip in that area.

Access: Mill Creek is accessible by automobile from the Abrams Falls parking area, the Becky Cable House, and the Forge Creek Road, all of which are off the Cades Cove Loop Road. The Forge Creek Road follows the upstream ascent of Forge Creek to 1,929 feet before leaving the stream.

An old, unmaintained road follows Mill Creek for 1 mile, after which there is no other trail access. The old road begins off the Forge Creek Road near the last crossing of Mill Creek.

Forge Creek is accessible from the Gregory Ridge Trail, which begins at the stream's last contact with the Forge Creek Road. This trail follows alongside the stream 2 miles, to 2,600 feet. The Ekaneetlee Manway offers access to Ekaneetlee Branch. This trail begins off the Gregory Ridge Trail behind the Big Poplar, which is about 2 miles from the trailhead. There is a backcountry campsite (#12, capacity 8), known as Ekaneetlee, .5 mile upstream on the trail. Note: The Ekaneetlee Manway is an unmaintained trail that should only be used by experienced hikers and trout fishermen.

Chapter 28

Minor Stream Systems of the Smokies

Besides the major watersheds, anglers may also fish a number of small streamsheds that begin within, but do not flow into, a larger system prior to departure from the park. They vary in size from hard-to-find Tabcat Creek, which flows from the extreme southern end of the park, to Parson Branch, a respectable-size creek with excellent auto access. Many of these little streams are seldom fished by anyone other than local anglers, although most offer fair to very good angling. These streams are broken down into two sections—Tennessee and North Carolina. Most should be considered early-season picks; it is not uncommon for these streams to shrink to little more than a trickle during the dry periods of summer.

TENNESSEE

Cosby Creek

> SIZE: Small
> FISHING PRESSURE: Moderate
> FISHING QUALITY: Fair
> ACCESS: TN 32, Cosby Campground Road; Cosby Creek Trail
> USGS QUADS: Luftee Knob, NC; Hartsford, TN

Few places in the Southern Appalachians compare with the colorful community of Cosby. In years past, this hilly hamlet laid a valid claim on the distinction of being the "Moonshine Capital of the World." Today, the storied cornmash distillery businessmen are difficult to locate, having forsaken running 'shine for other forms of livelihood.

Small, but productive, these seldom-visited creeks are true gems in the rough.

Cosby Creek is a small stream draining a surprisingly large basin bound by the lofty peaks of Mt. Cammerer and Mt. Inadu. The creek's lower reaches are populated by rainbow trout, while brookies still hold sway over the headwaters. This is one of the more scenic streams in the park, cascading over moss-encrusted boulders and passing under a canopy of hemlocks. Fishing quality is fair to poor where the creek flows past the Cosby Campground, a developed area offering 230 campsites. The middle and headwater reaches, including the tributaries of Crying Creek, Tom's Creek, Inadu Creek, and Rock Creek, offer slightly better opportunities.

Access: Cosby Creek flows under TN 32, 20 miles east of Gatlinburg, adjacent to the entrance to the park at the Cosby Campground Road. Upstream access from the park boundary to the campground is available via Cosby Campground Road, which travels alongside the creek.

The Cosby Creek Trail follows the stream after it leaves the road (the trailhead is located in the southeast corner of the Cosby Campground) for 1 mile before leaving the creek for the last time.

Indian Camp Creek

SIZE: Small
FISHING PRESSURE: Closed
FISHING QUALITY: Very good
ACCESS: Laurel Springs Road; Indian Camp Creek Trail
USGS QUADS: Jones Cove, TN; Mt. Guyot, TN

Indian Camp Creek, one of the most popular brookie streams in the park prior to the 1975 Brook Trout Moratorium, flows past nearby Albright Grove, where a magnificent virgin stand of poplars towers. Although Indian Camp Creek will probably remain closed to all fishing for some time, anglers are urged to make the 3-mile hike back to this wonderland to view the splendor of an uncut southern forest.

Access: The Indian Camp Creek Trail lends access to a portion of Indian Camp Creek. The trailhead is located off Laurel Springs Road, a gravel road that has a junction with TN 73 15.3 miles east of Gatlinburg. The trail crosses Cole Creek and Maddron Creek, tributaries of Indian Camp Creek, before reaching the main stream at 2.7 miles. Driving from Gatlinburg, as you pass the 15-mile mark, you will observe the Rainbow Ranch, a pay-to-fish pond on the right. Laurel Springs Road enters the highway near this establishment. The trailhead is a few hundred yards beyond.

Dunn Creek

SIZE: Small
FISHING PRESSURE: Closed
FISHING QUALITY: Good
ACCESS: TN 73
USGS QUADS: Jones Cove, TN; Mt. Guyot, TN

Six prongs of this lovely rivulet begin at an altitude of more than 4,400 feet among the steep slopes of Pinnacle Lead. Brook trout are still fairly common in the upper reaches of this little branch.

An old-timer from the Cosby community told me that at one time as many as fifteen moonshine stills operated along this branch and its prongs during the late 1940s.

Access: No maintained trails cross or follow the stream, although there was at one time an old path alongside it for several miles.

Webb Creek

SIZE: Small
FISHING PRESSURE: Light
FISHING QUALITY: Fair to questionable
ACCESS: TN 73
USGS QUADS: Jones Cove, TN; Mt. Guyot, TN-NC; Gatlinburg, TN

Webb Creek differs from the majority of waters described, because its flow within the Great Smoky Mountains National Park consists of several small brooks that later merge with the main stream outside the park. The main stream of Webb Creek leaves the park 13.5 miles east of Gatlinburg, passing under TN 73 as a small brook, having originated between the steep slopes of Snag Mountains and Pinnacle Lead. A number of very small feeder streams flowing out of the park pass under TN 73 to enter Webb Creek downstream from the park boundary. These streams include Texas Creek, a very small waterway with two prongs extending more than 4,000 feet in elevation; Nosy Creek, one of the largest of the feeder streams, with four prongs that each pass the 4,000-foot mark; Redwine Creek and Timothy Creek, both very small but lovely brooks; and Soak Ash Creek. Most of these waters have rainbow trout averaging less than 7 inches in length.

Access: Webb Creek is reached from the park boundary upstream only by moving along the trailless creek. The creek flows under TN 73, 13.5 miles east of Gatlinburg.

Hesse Creek

SIZE: Medium
FISHING PRESSURE: Light
FISHING QUALITY: Fair to good
ACCESS: Fairly remote
USGS QUADS: Kinel Springs, TN; Blockhouse, TN

Hesse Creek is the largest of the streams noted in this chapter, draining one of the most unique and least-visited regions of the Smokies. Hesse Creek Valley is often referred to as the Hurricane, probably because of severe blow-downs that have occurred here in the past.

The Hurricane is best known for its caves and unusual flora. Logged in the early part of the nineteenth century by the Little River Logging Company, Hesse Valley has today regrown nicely. One of the more unique items fishermen will notice are the lush canebrakes growing along the streams. The cane, actually a species of bamboo, *Arundinaria tecta*, was especially favored by old-time fishermen as excellent material for making fishing poles.

The quality of fishing in this watershed is fair to very good. There are plenty of trout here, although they average less than 8 inches in length. Noteworthy tributaries of Hesse Creek include Cane Creek and Bread Cane Creek.

Note: National Park Service regulations forbid the removal of any plant (or part thereof) from the park.

Access: There is no easy way to enter the Hurricane. All routes require a moderate amount of foot travel. Hesse Creek, upon leaving the Great Smoky Mountains National Park, flows through a lovely rural area known as Miller Cove. The Miller Cove Road (which has a junction with TN 73 near the intersection of the highway and the Foothills Parkway) dead-ends 1 mile from the park boundary. An old, unmaintained path continues upstream alongside Hesse Creek. Cane Creek (which originates in the park) enters the main stream at .7 mile from the right (another unmaintained path begins at its mouth, and follows the upstream ascent of Cane Creek, later having a junction with the Cooper Road Trail).

The path continues alongside Hesse Creek, entering the park at 1 mile, and at 1.3 miles arrives at the mouth of Bread Cane Creek. The Bread Cane Creek Trail follows alongside Bread Cane Creek to its headwaters, before terminating at 2.5 miles at the Cooper Road Trail. There are not trails upstream of Hesse Creek.

Tabcat Creek

SIZE: Small
FISHING PRESSURE: Light
FISHING QUALITY: Fair
ACCESS: Unnamed Path
USGS QUADS: Calderwood, TN-NC

Tabcat Creek is one of the least-known quality trout streams in the national park. Early spring is the best time to venture up this seldom-trampled stream, as it is quite small, and during the dry periods common to the late summer, it often appears to nearly dry up. Rainbow trout about 6 to 9 inches long are plentiful. Tributaries that can be fished include Bunker Hill Branch and Maynard Creek.

Access: Tabcat Creek flows into Calderwood Lake 2.5 miles south of the mouth of Abrams Creek on TN 72. There is an old, unmaintained path that begins at the park boundary, and follows Tabcat Creek to the confluence of Bunker Hill Branch, later reaching Bunker Hill.

Parson Branch

SIZE: Medium
FISHING PRESSURE: Relatively light
FISHING QUALITY: Fair
ACCESS: Parson Branch Road
USGS QUADS: Calderwood, TN-NC; Tapoco, TN-NC

Parson Branch is the sort of stream a trout fisherman passes on a Sunday drive with the family, and swears to return and fish later on, but never does. The stream holds a good population of rainbow trout, most of them fairly small. Black Gum Branch, a tributary of Parson Branch, also offers fair fishing.

Access: Parson Branch flows into Calderwood Lake after leaving the park. The Parson Branch Road, a one-way gravel road originating off the Cades Cove Loop Road, provides excellent roadside access to most of the main stream, following the stream from its headwaters to the park boundary.

NORTH CAROLINA

Chambers Creek

SIZE: Small
FISHING PRESSURE: Moderately light
FISHING QUALITY: Good
ACCESS: Remote
USGS QUADS: Noland Creek, NC

Chambers Creek offers fairly good trout fishing opportunities for those wishing to make the trip across Fontana Lake. There is an excellent backcountry campsite (Chambers Creek, #98, capacity 10) that serves fishermen nicely as a base camp. The stream is populated with rainbow trout, with brook trout reputed to be in the extreme headwater reaches. The North Fork and the West Fork merge .7 mile upstream from Fontana Lake, to form Chambers Creek. Both forks offer good trout fishing.

Access: Chambers Creek is located between Forney and Hazel creeks. It is most often visited by crossing Fontana Lake, and is easily recognized by the long cove that cushions it from the main body of the lake.

An unmaintained fisherman's trail ascends the creek. Upon reaching the junction of the North and West forks at .7 mile, the trail also forks, with footpaths following both small rivulets for a short distance.

Cooper Creek

SIZE: Small
FISHING PRESSURE: Light
FISHING QUALITY: Good
ACCESS: Cooper Creek Trail
USGS QUADS: Smokemont, NC

Cooper Creek is a noisy little rivulet tucked between two better-known watersheds, the Oconaluftee River and Deep Creek; it offers pretty fair angling for rainbow trout. Cooper Creek is relatively small, but those looking for an out-of-the-way locale in which to wet a line should not mark this little gem off their list.

Access: The Cooper Creek Trail offers good access to the most productive reaches of the stream. Its trailhead is located .4 mile upstream from the termination of the Cooper Creek Road, which has a junction with US 19 5.5 miles southwest of Cherokee.

The trail travels along the route of the stream 1.8 miles before leaving the creek. An unmaintained path continues alongside the stream for a distance.

Chapter 29

Fontana Lake

Perched almost 2,000 feet above sea level, Fontana Lake is one of the "highest" impoundments in the seven-state Tennessee Valley Authority (TVA). This 10,530-surface-acre lake sits wedged between the Great Smoky Mountains National Park and the Nantahala National Forest. During the summer, when the surrounding countryside is dominated by forest green and cloud-dotted pale blue skies, this emerald-green lake appears natural, sometimes giving the impression of being a jewel in a fine piece of jewelry.

Needless to say, Fontana Lake is a superbly scenic man-made lake. Development along this impoundment of the Tennessee River, although far from nonexistent, is limited. Several marinas sit on the lake's shoreline, offering the standard array of boat dock services (gas, snacks, boat rentals, launching ramp, and in some cases, guide services).

Physically, the lake gives the impression of greater altitude than its slightly less than 2,000 feet above sea level. There are no significant aquatic weeds here, and little in the way of fish-holding structure other than rock and gravel. The exceptions to this are the sites that are part of a fish attractor program carried out by TVA and North Carolina. This unique program establishes sites composed largely of man-made structures, usually in the form of downed trees or brush piles. These sites concentrate fish in numbers nine to nineteen times greater than along an unmanipulated shoreline.

Fontana Lake is a result of the impoundment of the Little Tennessee River which drains western North Carolina. The Little "T" River is formed by such well-known Carolina rivers as the Tuckasegee, Nantahala, and Oconaluftee. Primary feeder streams entering Fontana Lake along the north shore from the Great Smoky Mountains National Park are Eagle, Hazel, Chambers, Forney, and Noland creeks, while on the south shore the major

Smallies abound in Fontana Lake.

feeder streams entering from the Nantahala National Forest are Panther, Alarka and, and Stecoah creeks.

This is a storage-type impoundment that is drawn down more than 90 feet each season. The lake level is kept low during autumn and winter to accommodate potentially heavy seasonal rainfall. Lake levels begin to rise during early spring, with full pool (1,709-foot elevation maximum) usually achieved between May and July. A gradual drawdown usually begins in mid-to late July, although all the above water level data are dependent on annual rainfall, as well as power and downstream navigational needs.

Construction on Fontana Dam's began overnight following the United State's entrance into World War II in late 1941. The TVA was nearly ten years old when the Fontana project began, and had already begun a number of projects in the Tennessee River Valley. High-voltage power needs at defense plants in nearby Alcoa, Tennessee, for war plane production, as well as the then top-secret project taking shape in Oak Ridge, Tennessee (where the first atomic bomb was assembled), provided the impetus behind the dam's crash-building program.

Many thousands of acres of bottomland and ridge country were purchased from local residents, many of whom were less than willing to turn over family holdings to the federal government. Much of the acreage of these tracts became the lake and immediate ground, although 44,204 acres acquired from the mountain folk were later deeded over to the Great Smoky Mountains National Park. Today, this property forms the sometimes controversial north shore, Hazel Creek area. An additional 11,667 acres acquired along the lake's southern shoreline were later transferred to the U.S. Forest Service.

Less than a month after the bombing of Pearl Harbor, the first construction crews began arriving at the sleepy mountain hamlet known as Fontana Village. Legislation passed through Congress prior to the hostilities, for a dam atop the Little Tennessee River in Graham Country, North Carolina, had paved the way for the Fontana Lake project's beginning. This legislation was not adequate warning, though, for what was to ensue over the coming months. Survey crews arrived first, followed by building crews, who immediately began putting up housing for the soon-to-arrive seven thousand construction workers and support crews, who worked on the dam on a round-the-clock, twenty-four-hours-a-day, seven-days-a-week basis. To accommodate the influx of construction workers, engineers, support personnel, and their families, in addition to housing and dormitories, cafeterias, stores, laundries, and even movie houses and schools were built. The construction camp bore the name Fontana Village. Even during the war, when gas rationing and extremely poor mountain roads slowed most travel, more than one million Tennessee and North Carolina residents traveled here to witness the much-heralded building project.

Building Fontana Dam was an engineering accomplishment of astonishing merit. It ranks as the tallest dam east of the Rockies, standing 480 feet high from top to bottom, yet it took only slightly more than two years to complete this remote dam. The project's cost was only seventy-one million dollars, a mere fraction of what such a gigantic undertaking would cost today!

The completed Fontana Dam construction project left TVA with a new, ready-to-operate hydroelectric/flood control facility, and a white elephant construction ghost town. Even before the project's completion, federal and state officials had realized Fontana Village's recreational possibilities. The war years were, unfortunately, an inopportune time to kick off a tourism project, and for several years only dam maintenance crews resided here.

A number of tourist oriented corporations have operated Fontana Village. Since the late 1980s Pepper Ridge Inc., has run the Fontana Village complex for TVA. Personally, my family and I have stayed at Fontana Village many times over the years, and have made return trips to the quaint, low-development area an annual event. Two things about Fontana Village make it different from virtually all other southern Appalachian vacation spots. First, much of the rustic nature found here when Fontana Village was a backwoods construction camp still exists. The worker cabins and cottages have been remodeled, and are now guest lodging, but their rough-hewn character still glimmers through. The old cafeteria still serves up homemade fruit pies and biscuits'n'gravy, as it did daily forty years ago; the old movie house that once flickered Bogie and John Wayne movies across its silver screen still shows the latest movies. Modern amenities abound, but much of the village's former self is openly visible. In recent years, Fontana Village has hosted many movie-making companies. The last time I was there, Jodie Foster was making "Nell," and Dan Ackroyd and Jack Lemmon were also filming there.

Fontana Village's other unique attribute is its locale and proximity to the finest treasure house of the Southern highlands. One has only to walk a few hundred feet from any point here to enjoy the region's lush flora. The Appalachian Trail passes directly through the village, and other trails and noteworthy backcountry destinations are easily reached from this place.

When staying here, the area's low-key approach and total lack of competing development give one a strong feeling of having stepped back in time fifty years.

Fishing is without question Fontana Lake's number-one drawing card. Angling is nearly always very good here, although to be perfectly honest this could very well be the tough fly-fishing water in the world. The lake's setting amidst such splendid mountains makes even those certain-to-occur fishless days easy to swallow, and this is good, as much of the time the prime game fish quarries are deeper than most fly-fishermen can effectively fish.

Fontana Lake sports a surprisingly diverse game fish fishery for a mountain lake. Angling for smallmouth bass, walleye, white bass, rainbow and steelhead trout, muskie and tiger muskie, and bream is on a par with that of lakes anywhere. Catfish are also plentiful, and fishing for largemouth bass, brown trout, red breast bream, and crappie rates fair to good.

Much of Fontana Lake's nationally recognized fishing reputation grew around this lake's smallmouth bass fishery. While everyone has their own opinion of which game fish is the top battler when stung by a hook (and I might add I am a dyed- in-the-wool trout fisherman), most angling surveys end with the smallmouth bass at the top of the list—and rightfully so! The acrobatics these chunky, muscle-bound fish go through each time they are hooked are enough to inspire even the most jaded trout fisherman.

Fontana Lake, with its steep, rocky shoreline and year-round cool water temperatures, is picture-perfect bronzeback habitat. Bronzebacks in the 10- to 14-inch class are the usual fare, but 3 pound smalljaws are always a possibility, and tackle busters in the 4- to 6- and even 7-pound class inhabit every rocky point.

The best smallmouth bass fishing occurs between mid-April and late June. This time slot encompasses the smallies' early-season awakening. Movement into small feeder creek areas takes place first, followed by the nesting time along the gravel shoreline areas.

When these fish are found in these areas, fly rods strung with sinking fly lines enable you to offer large wet flies, as well as larger streamers such as a Muddler Minnow, which are highly effective.

Hot weather and "long-day sunshine" send the smallmouth bass deep in the lake from July through September, with average depths being 10 to 35 feet deep during the daylight hours. When these fish are this deep they can still be caught on streamers taken to the correct depth by utilizing high density, sinking lines. Because deep-structure fishing with these bottom-chunking baits is difficult and usually frustrating for inexperienced anglers, many Fontana Lake bass fishermen turn to the twilight hours, when the brown bass return to the shallows to feed.

Nighttime smallmouth and largemouth bass fly-fishing here can be outstanding. Surface-worked hair flies and popping bugs are extremely effective.

Largemouth bass are readily available throughout Fontana Lake, even though this impoundment is seldom touted for its green hawg fishery. Granted, the largemouth bass are not caught as frequently as the smalljaws, but they are actively sought.

Fly-fishing techniques used to take Fontana's bronzebacks are solid ploys for "ole bucket mouth." Holding areas for both are closer than on most lakes that hold both smallmouth and largemouth bass, due to this lake's steep walls. There are a few mud flats in the headwaters (which are preferred by the warmer-natured largemouth bass during the spring) but generally speaking, these fish are lumped into the same general areas, which in turn makes the tactics and baits used for the bronzeback quite effective for its larger-growing cousin as well.

Fontana Lake has a long-standing reputation as an outstanding walleye fishery. These large-growing perch were native to the Little "T" River drainage prior to this lake's creation, and have prospered well here. Late winter finds these river-spawning fish in the swift headwaters of the Little "T," Nantahala, and Tuckasegee rivers. Trampling the riverbanks while casting green or yellow streamers along the rocky bottom is the best way to catch a mess of spawning-run marble-eyes.

Many anglers visit this lake to explore its little-touted trout fishery. Rainbow trout originally descended Fontana's well-known trout streams—Hazel, Noland, and Forney—while subsequent stockings of these fish have resulted in a first-class lake rainbow trout fishery. Recent introduction of steelhead rainbow trout by North Carolina fishery managers has provided a relatively new fishery for these "sea run" 'bows, which hopefully will achieve greater growth than the stream-oriented rainbows common to Fontana's open-water environment. The lake also contains a little-fished-for and generally overlooked brown trout population.

Late winter and early spring find these cold-natured exotics in the headwaters of the lake's numerous feeder streams. This is spawning time for these trout (except the browns), and swift-moving water is required for mating success. While actual spawning takes place upstream from the lake (see the chapters on Hazel, Forney, Eagle, and Noland creeks), good rainbow trout catches always occur in the creek mouths, where these fish "stage" in large numbers prior to ascending the current.

Large, brightly colored streamers and large, gaudy wet flies drift fished and stripped are effective. You'll need sinking tips or high-density sinking line to accomplish this. During late winter and spring, these fish are not overly aggressive, but persistence and keeping your bait wet will usually undo the reluctance of these fish. Most trout caught from Fontana Lake average 12 to 16 inches, but trout are commonly taken in excess of 5 pounds!

Fontana Lake's trout become roamers during the summer and autumn months, frequenting open water and large creek embayments. Hot weather sends trout deep, up to 50 feet down during the dog days.

One of the most popular and abundant game fish found in this highland lake is the white bass. Each spring, during April, nearly everyone stops fishing for black bass, walleye, and trout to make trips to the headwaters to cash in on the white bass's river spawning run. Daily catches in excess of a hundred white bass, or stripe as most locals refer to these true bass, are common.

The North Carolina state record white bass, a compact 4-pound, 15-ounce specimen, was taken from Fontana Lake in 1966. When early-spring water temperatures reach the mid-fifties, these gregarious 2- to 3-pound fish ascend from the lake to spawn in the Tuckasegee, Little "T," and Nantahala rivers. Small white, yellow, or green streamers are deadly river-run white bass baits.

River-spawning whites are aggressive fish that station themselves in the shoals and pools. Casting across the current and briskly retrieving your offering is the favorite method. Fly-fishermen can have great fun using bright streamers and weight-forward sinking line.

During the rest of the year, the lake's white bass roam the open water in great schools, ripping up shallow shad schools. These fish remain shallow (2 to 15 feet deep) throughout the hot-weather months. Top-water action using bass bugs can be fun when the whites are in the "jumps," feeding on surface shad.

Bluegill and redbreast bream are probably the most sought-after vacation-time fish species in Fontana Lake. Naturally, popping bugs are the way for flyrodders to go after these gamesters. During the spring these fish are generally concentrated in extreme back-cove areas under shoreline debris. During the late June/July bream nesting period, shallow backwater areas are sought out. For late-summer "trophy" bluegill action, try using wet flies (7 to 15 feet deep) along main channel cliffs and rock bluffs. Stringing your fly rod with a high density fly line and using a Zug Bug (sizes No.8 to No.10) will give you some great bluegill action.

Camping is popular around Fontana Lake. Backcountry camping is permitted along the north shore in the Great Smoky Mountains National Park on a permit basis. This is "tent only" camping, and only a limited number of people per site are permitted. These campsites include Lost Cove along the Eagle Creek embayment, Proctor along the Hazel Creek embayment, Kirkland Creek at the mouth of Kirkland Creek, Hicks Branch between Kirkland and the mouth of Chambers Creek, Chambers Creek along the Chambers Creek embayment, Lower Forney along the Forney Creek embayment, Goldmine Branch along the Goldmine Branch embayment, and Lower Noland Creek inland along the narrow Noland Creek embayment. These campsites are popular, and are often full. Also, many are readily accessible by boat only when the lake is at full pool.

The U.S. Forest Service maintains two well-developed campgrounds along Fontana Lake's southern shoreline. Cable Cove Campground, located near the mouth of Rattlesnake Branch and accessible from US 19 approximately 2 miles east of Fontana Village, offers boat access, sanitary facilities, and trailer spaces. Tsali Campground, located in the lake's Little Tennessee River arm, offers the same services. Both are well maintained and highly recommended.

Chapter 30

The Finger Lakes
of the Smokies

Wine connoisseurs fond of New York State white and sparkling wines probably believe the United States's only "finger lakes" are those glacial afterthoughts found in the Empire State. Not so, and if you don't believe this, just look at the Great Smoky Mountains National Park's southern edge.

Found here are three slender, snaking lakes: Cheoah, Calderwood, and Chilhowee, the Finger Lakes of the South. Unlike nearly all other nearby man-made lakes in the Tennessee River drainage, this string of Little Tennessee River impoundments is not part of the gigantic Tennessee Valley Authority system. Each is owned and operated by Tapoco, a subsidiary of the Aluminum Company of America (or Alcoa).

These are old impoundments. Cheoah Dam was completed in 1919; Calderwood was finished and ready to operate in 1930; and Chilhowee was finished in 1959. Being located between the Great Smoky Mountains National Park and Nantahala and Cherokee national forests (as well as corporate properties) has served to make development along these lakes virtually nonexistent. There are no marinas, no restaurants, no gas stations, and only a very, very few lodging stations near the lakes' collective 27-mile length alongside US 129 and US 19. While this is certainly an inconvenience of sorts for some, the lakes' surrounding raw nature is a solace for most.

All three impoundments have scenic qualities rarely found in the handiwork of humans, and more important to anglers, each holds loads of brightly silvered trout. It would be easy to lump these lakes together, but each differs from the others in a variety of ways.

Sound interesting? You bet it is!

Great fly fishing is found in the "trash lines" that form below these dams.

Cheoah Lake

Cheoah was the first impoundment built on the Little Tennessee River, predating the creation of the Tennessee Valley Authority by almost fifteen years. The dam's hydroelectric-producing capabilities are quite substantial despite its age, with the bulk of its production power consumed by Alcoa for the production of aluminum. This old dam is visible where US 129 crosses Calderwood Lake near Tapoco. An interesting side note on this structure—it was the site of the famous "dam jump" scene in the 1994 movie "The Fugitive."

Cheoah Lake extends approximately 10 miles behind 189-foot-high Cheoah Dam. Despite the dam's impressive height, much of the lake is silt-filled, with its winding main channel and the area near the Santeetlah Powerhouse being the lake's deepest zones.

The Finger Lake area along the Little Tennessee River was one of the primary cultural centers of the Overhill Cherokee. These tribes were forcibly removed from the eastern United States during the late 1830s. By the time of the Civil War, this area was completely settled, although it was never crowded. The Little Tennessee River's course was a natural route for railways, and logging trains made daily treks out this way by the end of the nineteenth century. Only the rising water from these lakes halted timber operations in a number of otherwise remote watersheds. Today this area is fully forested, and displays a wild look seldom found around man-made lakes.

Beginning beneath the concrete walls of Fontana Lake, Cheoah is fed year-round with cold, clean water. This fact makes Cheoah Lake one of the coldest, if not the coldest, impoundments south of the Mason-Dixon Line.

Trout are the lake's primary game fish, and this lake is stocked regularly by the state of North Carolina with rainbow, brown, and brook trout. Although food is not as abundant for the trout here as in Fontana, Cheoah's trout grow reasonably fast, and this lake environment allows them to achieve large sizes. Twelve- to 16-inch rainbows and browns are common, and larger browns up to 5 to 7 pounds are available in good numbers. The brookies usually do not grow longer than a foot, but by Southern stream standards this is large.

Cheoah Lake's major feeder streams are Lewellyn Branch, a small tributary that enters the lake near the US 19 bridge, and Twenty Mile Creek, a major stream that enters four miles upstream from Cheoah Dam. Both drain the high country in the Great Smoky Mountains National Park.

Icy water from Santeetlah Lake several miles away, yet connected to Cheoah Lake via a pipeline, descends 663 feet before emptying at the Santeetlah Powerhouse, approximately 5.4 miles upstream from Cheoah Dam.

Cheoah Lake begins immediately downstream from Fontana Dam's tailrace, and accounts for approximately 595 surface acres. Unlike upstream Fontana and most other western Carolina highland impoundments, Cheoah is not a storage-type reservoir. Its limit capacity is quickly achieved whenever Fontana Dam's hydroelectric turbines are in operation. Extended periods of upstream power generation automatically mean reciprocal turbine activity at Cheoah Dam.

Cheoah's headwaters are actually a tailrace river, and are very productive during brief periods following turbine shutdowns at Fontana Dam. There is something magical about a tailrace river's descent following shutoffs. Aquatic insects (although scant) emerge, regardless of the time of day, and trout seem to come out of the woodwork. Fly-fishing streamers, dries, or nymphs works well.

Limited natural reproduction occurs each spring in the Twenty Mile Creek drainage area. At this time, many successful anglers concentrate their efforts along this narrow embayment and in fishing near the bottom.

Shoreline fishing is very popular during the spring, particularly near the Twenty Mile Creek embayment and the Santeetlah Powerhouse, as well as along the highly accessible ways of US 129 and US 19.

There are no commercial docks or launches on Cheoah Lake, but there are two unnamed public launch ramps. The first, and most popular, is located on the north shore just down the lake from the US 19 bridge. The second is located at the Santeetlah Powerhouse, which is accessible from Tapoco via US 129. To reach the Santeetlah Powerhouse area, travel south on US 129 from its split with US 19, cross Calderwood Lake, and turn left onto Meadow Branch Road. At approximately 4 miles, this gravel road arrives at the Santeetlah Powerhouse and ramp.

Tapoco is a very small outpost, primarily operated for Tapoco employees, families, and support personnel. Scona Lodge, a historical mountain hideaway, is located here, and although several attempts have been made to reopen this quaint, turn-of-the-cen-

Big trout are common in these seldom-fished lakes.

tury establishment, at this writing I am sorry to say it is closed, with no reopening in the foreseeable future.

Camping is permitted along the lake's southern shoreline, which is held jointly by Tapoco and the Nantahala National Forest. Extended stays of more than ten days are not advised, nor is littering, cutting down green or dead trees, and other related behavior. Many areas along the lake's southern shoreline are accessible only by boat, and make a stay here quite pleasurable.

Calderwood Lake

Calderwood Lake is one of the South's least-known gems. Located between Cheoah and Chilhowee on the Little "T," this 536-acre impoundment offers superb trout fishing. Unlike its upstream counterpart, Cheoah Lake, Calderwood offers more angling opportunities than just trout.

Bream fishing along the shoreline in Calderwood's lower end can be explosive during the summer months. Nymphs fished 1 to 4 feet deep are effective, but if your tastes are a bit more difficult to stimulate, try using a popping bug.

Calderwood Dam stands 213 feet high, but is less than 200 feet across. During the summer, this arch-shaped dam has the visual impact of a concrete wedge driven between two green sofa pillows. The lake is deep, with depths more than 190 feet in the lower end along the river channel, which winds over 8 miles back through rugged, remote ridges.

Like Cheoah, Calderwood Lake fluctuates, usually on a daily basis. The lake's level is dependent upon upstream generating activity. Cheoah River enters the lake at its headwaters only a few hundred feet downstream from Cheoah Dam, although the two are unrelated.

Santeetlah Lake is created by the impoundment of the Cheoah River. If you're not confused now, add to this the fact that although the Cheoah River resurfaces downstream from Santeetlah Lake and is a "textbook" tailrace flow, it is not affected by power generated using Santeetlah Lake's stored water. This is accomplished at the Santeetlah Powerhouse on the south shore of Cheoah Lake.

Cheoah River drains a large section of the Nantahala National Forest. Other key feeder streams include Parsons Branch, a medium-size trout stream draining the Great Smoky Mountains National Park, and Slickrock Creek, one of North Carolina and Tennessee's premier brown trout streams. This stream's 10,700-acre watershed is shared by the Cherokee and Nantahala national forests, and is protected by the U.S. Wilderness System.

The Tennessee/North Carolina state line bisects this lake less than 2 miles downstream from Cheoah Dam. A long-standing reciprocle agreement between these two adjoining states honors both states' fishing licenses on the entire lake and Slickrock Creek.

The lake's northern shoreline is National Park Service domain, and there is no roadside camping or designated backcountry campsite along Calderwood's length. The lake's southern shore is shared by the U.S. Forest Service (Nantahala and Cherokee national forests) and Tapoco. Camping is permitted for reasonable lengths of time, and under relatively liberal restraints on both properties, although commonly acknowledged courtesies such as no littering, permanent structures, large fires, cutting of standing timber, etc., are required of those using these properties.

Calderwood Lake is the most remote and difficult to access of the Smoky Mountains Finger Lakes. Roadside access from US 129 is only available immediately downstream from Cheoah Dam at the two-lane highway's intersection with a gravel road which leads off US 129 to Calderwood Dam. The latter is a steep roadway, difficult to pass during inclement weather. There are no marinas or other facilities on this lake.

Fishing pressure on Calderwood is light. Both Tennessee and North Carolina fishery departments stock this lake with brook, rainbow, and brown trout. Food for the trout is in short supply, but because fishing pressure is also scant, many of the lake's stocked trout live out their lives achieving considerable size. Brown or rainbow trout in excess of 10 pounds are taken each year.

This is a bit ironic to those old-timers who remember when Calderwood Lake was created during the 1930s. At that time, fishery folks believed such high-elevation lakes could only be sterile, oxygen-depressed deserts, and this notion was carried over well into the TVA era. When Norris Lake was constructed during the mid-1930s, warm water fish species hatcheries were also built to "hopefully establish some sort of fishery" in that 35,000-acre lake.

Following the impoundment of the Little Tennessee River at Calderwood Lake, no one checked to see if fish could exist in the lake—no one except the local fishermen, who discovered that trout from the tributary mountain stream had migrated into the lake, where they were growing fast and fat. For almost ten years, the secret of this lake's excellent trout fishing was kept by a small group of anglers. When it was discovered that trout could live in tailrace rivers and deep mountain impoundments, regular stocking began here. To the chagrin of many local anglers, the quality of this lake's trout fishery actually dropped (in their opinion), due to the planting of fish from locales other than the mountain streams!

Fly-fishing for trout at Calderwood Lake is very much like fly-fishing for trout at Cheoah, except during the summer these fish are deeper, often requiring the use of a high-density sinking line, particularly in the lake's lower end. Night fishing in the lake's upper third is also popular and highly productive, not to mention being lots of fun. One word to the wise: Even on the hottest August nights, you can catch a nasty head cold in this frigid ravine!

Trout are very shallow at times or, for reasons unknown to this scribe, very deep. During the spring, dry flies and terrestrial patterns are productive along the abundantly tree-lined shore. Seeing a 4-pound rainbow cartwheeling through a blooming redbud tree will certainly get your attention if the beautiful scenery around this highland lake hasn't already.

Chilhowee Lake

The third "Finger Lake" is Chilhowee, a 1,747-acre impoundment of the Little Tennessee River, and the only body of water in this group solely in Tennessee. Until the late 1970s, Chilhowee Lake was the final indignation borne by the Little "T" before emptying into the Tennessee River just downstream from Fort Loudoun Dam.

At that time, what was thought by many to be the finest trout river in the eastern United States was spawned beneath the shadow of Chilhowee Dam. Brown trout weighing more than 7 pounds were common, as growth rates were excellent due to the rich limestone base over which the tailrace river flowed.

During the 1960s, TVA began the Tellico Project, and despite desperate efforts on the part of fishermen, conservationists, the Cherokee Nation, and others to stop and stall this endeavor, the project progressed and mournfully became a reality.

During the late 1960s, the famed snail darter was discovered in the Little "T" tailrace below Chilhowee Dam, and at that time was not known to exist in any other waters. This 3-inch perch was quickly added to the federal Endangered Species Act list, and for a time was both hailed and damned for halting this project. Ultimately, though, a slick congressional move by a Knoxville congressman permitted the Endangered Species Act to be sidestepped, and the freshly completed gates at Tellico Dam were closed, drowning forever this outstanding trout river. Many fishermen will long remember this majestic flow, which accounted for half of Tennessee's total trout water surface acreage.

I last fished that river only two weeks before it was killed. It was a bright autumn day, and we arrived just as the turbines at Chilhowee Dam were shut down. Our party of four caught almost 300 trout, releasing many fish over 19 inches long. It was a golden farewell to a 24-carat trout river.

Chilhowee Lake is the most diverse, accessible, and popular of the Finger Lakes. The dam stands only 68 feet high, but it backs up a lake over 9 miles long. At its widest point, Chilhowee Lake is almost a mile across; five times wider than either Calderwood or Cheoah at their widest points.

This is a remarkably shallow mountain lake, seldom topping more than 50 feet deep, and usually less than 20, with 10-foot-deep water being very abundant along the shoreline. Chilhowee's headwaters are wedged between two vertical rock cliffs well worth boating up the lake to view.

Chilhowee Lake's primary feeder streams are Tallassee Creek, which enters along the south shore, draining the Cherokee National Forest; Tabcat Creek, a minor Great Smoky Mountains National Park stream that creates a nice embayment area approximately 5 miles upstream from the dam; and Abrams Creek, a major Great Smoky Mountains National Park stream that enters the lake 3 miles upstream from the dam, resulting in a large embayment of Abrams and Panther creeks.

Chilhowee is actually two lakes: one is the cold-water trout fishery located in the lake's upper half, and the other a warm-water lake beginning around the mouth of Tabcat Creek. The cold-water fishery is maintained by the regular influx of icy, clean water from upstream Calderwood Dam.

Trolling for trout is popular and productive, as is night trout fishing, which is practiced here just as on the upstream lakes, although by greater numbers of anglers. During the summer, the lake is alive with lights, as all sorts of fishing and pleasure crafts dot its course vying for tasty trout.

Fly-fishermen will be delighted to discover that this lake offers season-long summertime long rod trout action in the trash line. Trash, or debris, lines beginning at the base of Calderwood Dam form from shoreline to shoreline. Viewed from above, these trash lines resemble "bathtub rings" as they slowly wash down the lake, disappearing approximately 5 miles downstream.

These so-called trash lines hold large numbers of beetles, bees, and other terrestrial foods that are of considerable interest to Chilhowee Lake's big rainbow trout. Trout cruise these trash lines, gingerly picking off insects. Fly flickers using large nymphs or beetle patterns sit in the bow of their boat or canoe, and watch the lake's mirror-like surface for an approaching feeder.

Once a trout begins prowling a debris line, it will follow it from one end to the other, rhythmically surfacing every 10 to 20 feet.

Few waters are more tranquil than the Finger Lakes of the Smokies.

The trick is to gauge your quarry's surface pattern and attempt to drop your fly where the fish will probably surface next. Admittedly, this is a hit-or-miss angling technique, but it can be very effective. One nearby Maryville fly-fisherman who has been flicking to the trash line trout for many years confided he took over thirty trout in excess of 20 inches from Chilhowee Lake in a single month!

Bluegill and catfish are abundant along the lake's lower half shoreline. Natural baits are the most popular way of taking these fish. Chilhowee Lake is an excellent largemouth bass lake, although it is seldom noted as such. While fishing here in 1983, I saw one angler hook into a 7-inch stocked trout one afternoon, only to have a 10-pound hawg engulf the panicked trout. The bass was successfully landed by the fisherman.

Most bass fishing takes place downstream from the Tabcat Creek launch area. Little fishing takes place here during cold weather.

Chilhowee Lake sports no marinas, but it does have three public boat launch areas. The first is located at the mouth of Abrams Creek, the second is located one mile upstream from the first, and the third is located at the mouth of Tabcat Creek, 5 miles upstream from the dam. All three are easily visible from US 129.

Camping is permitted on the lake's south shore, on properties owned by Tapoco and the Cherokee National Forest. Camping also occurs on the north shore downstream from the Panther Creek embayment area, but I cannot recommend this for two reasons. One, the area is gravel covered and virtually void of trees or other vegetation; and two, this area is frequented by thugs, hoods, and other unsavory sorts. I am at home around these gents and lasses, but anyone buying this book might certainly be otherwise.

Map Data

There are no individual maps of Cheoah, Calderwood, and Chilhowee lakes. A good map depicting Fontana and the Finger Lakes is available from TVA by writing the TVA Map Sales; Haney Building; Chattanooga, TN 37401. USGS quadrangles of these lakes are as follows: Cheoah Lake—Fontana Dam, NC, Tapoco, NC; Calderwood Lake—Tapoco, NC, Calderwood, NC; Chilhowee Lake—Calderwood, NC.

Chapter 31

Cherokee Indian Reservation Public Trout Fishing

The public trout-fishing streams of the Eastern Band of the Cherokee Indian Nation in western North Carolina, adjacent to the Great Smoky Mountains National Park, rate among the most intensely managed waters in the United States. A total of 30 stream miles designated as "Enterprise Waters" by tribal leaders flow through the Qualla Reservation, and annually provide thousands of fishermen with fun and trout.

Enterprise Waters are stocked twice weekly during the regular season (April through October) and weekly during the winter season (November through February). Creel-size (8 to 12 inches) rainbow, brook, and brown trout constitute the bulk of the Cherokee's regular stocking efforts. However, just to keep things interesting, each week trophy-class 3- to 12-pound trout are released in all these waters. The present North Carolina state record brook trout, a 7-pound, 7-ounce beauty, was taken in 1980 from the Enterprise Waters portion of Raven Creek.

In addition to offering excellent fly-fishing for all three species of trout, the waters of Qualla Reservation also hold a bevy of large smallmouth and tons of hand-size rock bass. These fish are exceedingly common in the lower reaches of the Oconaluftee River as well as downstream from its mouth at the Tuckasegee River.

The Qualla Reservation's trout fishing quality rates high. Summer creel limits are liberal: ten trout per day. Bait restrictions during this popular time slot are also virtually nonexistent. Naturally, the creation of such a worm-dunk paradise bears a price tag.

Visitors are charged daily and seasonal user fees, but presently anglers fishing here are exempt from needing a state fishing or trout license. All things considered, the cost of fishing at Qualla is

Tribal waters open to the public can be fly-fished year-round.

a red-hot bargain, especially if you're fishing for the frying pan or a trophy trout.

Revenue from fishing permit sales allows the tribe's fishery personnel to stock tens of thousands of trout annually. Until 1983 the Qualla Reservation was largely dependent on hatchery production from sources other than their own, primarily federal. Closure of a number of federal hatcheries forced the construction of a tribal fishery, which is located adjacent to Raven Fork on the Big Cove Road.

The tribe's three ponds open to the public are of interest, especially to those with young children or those unable to scamper around the rock-strewn creek banks. These ponds account for six surface acres, and are located beside Big Cove Road, approximately 5 miles upstream from the town of Cherokee. They are encircled by well-manicured fescue grass, and are heavily stocked twice weekly. The three ponds are both productive and popular.

Several seasons ago, during the winter, I had been fly-fishing Raven Fork upstream from the pond, where I'd limited out on 12- to 15-inch trout before returning to town via Big Cove Road by these ponds. Only one car could be seen in the gravel parking area there. Approaching that lonely vehicle were three frail-looking elderly women and one man. Each woman carried a rod and reel, but their male companion was burdened with what was without question the most impressive stringer of trout I have ever seen. On that stringer were sixteen rainbow trout weighing between three and seven pounds each. Naturally, I stopped to goggle and asked the expected question: "Whatcha catch 'em on?" One of the ladies produced her rod tip, which held a single shanked hook with the body portion of a yellow jelly grub. Rubberized corn 'n pond trout—the bane of me yet!

While bait fishing is rampant on these waters, fly-fishing is still legal. Actually, fly-fishing is remarkably good here. Higher fertility results in better hatches of aquatic insects than in the national park. The presence of the sometimes pesky "stockers" does not adversely affect the resident population of trout, which is in surprisingly good condition according to tribal fishery experts. Fly patterns and techniques outlined for fly-fishing national park waters work extremely well on these tribal waters.

Streams presently under the Qualla Reservation's Enterprise Waters designation include: Raven Fork downstream from its confluence with Straight Fork; Bunches Creek downstream from where it passes under the gravel road; the Oconaluftee River from its entrance into the Qualla Reservation, downstream to its boundary at Birdstown; and Soco Creek downstream from its confluence with Hornbuckle Creek, to its mouth at the Oconaluftee River. All of these flows are tributaries of the Oconaluftee River and, with the exception of Soco Creek, all begin within the pristine confines of the Great Smoky Mountains National Park.

Raven Fork

SIZE: Medium to fairly large

FISHING PRESSURE: Extremely heavy

FISHING QUALITY: Very good for stocked trout, outstanding odds for trophy-class trout

ACCESS: Big Cove Road

USGS QUADS: Smokemont, NC; Bunches Bald, NC; Whittier, NC

Raven Fork leaves the Great Smoky Mountains National Park as more than a mountain rill; it rates as a small, fast-flowing river in its own right. This is one of the more popular "put'n'take" streams, but one which, surprisingly, hosts a smart native population of rainbow and brown trout, which many anglers overlook for the easier-to-catch food hatchery trout.

Raven Fork's upstream Qualla Reservation reaches are reserved for enrolled members of the Eastern Band of Cherokee Indians, but public fishing is welcomed downstream from the creek's confluence with Straight Fork.

Big Cove Road, which begins at its junction with US 441 in the town of Cherokee, quickly traces alongside Raven Fork from its mouth at the Oconaluftee River to the starting point of the Enterprise Waters at the mouth of Straight Fork, a distance of approximately 8 miles. Big Cove Road is an excellent paved highway, with a liberal scattering of commercial campgrounds and stores along its route.

While Raven Fork is a moderately wide, fast stream with an abundance of medium to shallow riffles, it also sports a large number of cascades and corresponding deep plunge pools.

Aesthetically, the Qualla Reservation portion of Raven Fork does not have the pristine, unspoiled splendor of its upstream national park headwaters. In all truthfulness, none of the heavily trampled Enterprise Waters are as pleasing to the eye as those in the national park. This is not to say that Raven Fork or the other Cherokee waters are not scenic, because they certainly are. However, complete protection is not afforded these streams, and signs of usage can be found.

It is worth noting that 90 percent of Raven Fork (and other Enterprise Waters) flows very close alongside roadways that lend easy access.

There is a truism that also covers the stocking truck's twice-weekly deliveries. Newcomers curious as to where most of the best-stocked waters are located can make a "crack'o'dawn" drive along any Enterprise Waters. Crowds, which always contain a cadre of regular long rods, will give you a blueprint to follow for future trips.

Should you make such a drive, you will quickly see that less than 10 percent of the available water receives 90 percent of the angling pressure. Those lonely roadside ripples and apparently unproductive shallow runs are fished, but usually during secondary time slots, that is, when results are suboptimal.

First, those areas void of crowds are usually not stocked as heavily, particularly those areas well off the road. In the out-of-the-way gorge-type runs, a certain amount of natural dispersal occurs, regularly bringing trout into these out-of-the-way locales. While some trouters disdain stocked trout, all will acknowledge that the longer a stocker survives in its new home, the more stream savvy it acquires, and the more difficult it becomes to dupe onto a hook.

Raven Fork possesses a fair number of such remote, steep-banked gorges, that require considerable effort to get into. These areas are not usually stocked, but they hold amazing concentrations of sizable trout, particularly angler-wary browns.

Personally, I am uncomfortable fly-fishing in a crowd, or for that matter being in any crowd, be it in a liquor store or on a trout stream. Solitude is available on Raven Fork's off-the-beaten-path reaches, but do not expect easy pickin's because Cherokee's trout streams receive considerable angling pressure, and you are probably not the only fisherman who's drifted a night crawler along a difficult-to-access reach in recent memory.

One additional word of advice on the off-the-beaten-path stream reaches. Naturally, you will want to try the most likely-looking runs and pools; everyone does. But if you want to up your catch rate, ferret your bait around unlikely-looking bankside structure and shallow midstream areas. Holdover trout many times become such creatures simply by virtue of taking up overlooked holding stations.

Bunches Creek

SIZE: Medium to small
FISHING PRESSURE: Heavy
FISHING QUALITY: Excellent
ACCESS: Bunches Creek Road, (a four-wheel-drive-only gravel road)
USGS QUADS: Bunches Bald, NC

Bunches Creek is a medium-sized tributary to Raven Fork, and flows into the latter at the junction of Big Cove Road and Bunches Creek Road, a rough, four-wheel-drive-vehicle-only gravel road that connects Big Cove Road with the Blue Ridge Parkway, then on to US 19. That section of Bunches Creek downstream from the creek's last contact with the road (approximately 3.6 miles from its mouth) to its junction with Raven Fork is open to the public as Enterprise Waters.

Bunches Creek is one of Cherokee's most overlooked little trout-fishing hotspots. It is a small creek, but a very lovely bit of moving water. A constant overstory of hemlocks and hickories and a lack of crowds make this one ideal for fly-fishermen seeking a bit of elbow room.

Bunches Creek has several noteworthy tributaries, most of which begin within the National Park, although not all by any means. These include Indian Creek (shown as Redman Creek on older maps), which begins at more than 5,000 feet in elevation west of the Heintooga Overlook on the western slopes of the Balsam Mountains in the park, and enters Bunches Creek approximately 1.3 miles upstream from its mouth. An old jeep road traces alongside Indian Creek, but under present tribal regulations, this stream is not open to public fishing.

Heintooga Creek, another high-elevation park flow, enters Bunches Creek approximately 2.4 miles upstream. This stream begins in the craggy area between Horsetrough and Heintooga ridges on the Balsam Mountains range. It is a pretty hop-across stream, which enters Bunches Creek at an elevation of almost 3,000 feet. Although the regulations given out by the Qualla Reservation Game and Fish Management Enterprise do not show this stream, it is restricted to tribal members only.

Oconaluftee River

SIZE: Large
FISHING PRESSURE: Extremely heavy, but rarely crowded
FISHING QUALITY: Superb, particularly for large trout
ACCESS: US 441; Big Cove Road
USGS QUADS: Whittier, NC; Bryson City, NC

Fishing the reservation's reaches of the Oconaluftee River is a treat, and would be so even if it were not intensively stocked. This is one of the eastern U.S.'s great brown trout streams, and one that shells out huge, full-finned "resident" trout with as much regularity as many western streams.

The Oconaluftee River is large enough to float fish from a canoe or johnboat during most seasons, although surprisingly few anglers use these crowd-beating methods. Most float trips occur downstream from the river's US 19 bridge.

Upon leaving the national park, the Oconaluftee River bisects the bustling tourist town of Cherokee, the Qualla Reservation's tribal center. Although you might be casting a Light Cahill in the shadow of a hamburger emporium, this does not really matter when the fish are biting. The river's roar and the delight of fishing bury all thoughts of civilization.

Fishing pressure is most intense where access is easiest: upstream from the US 19W bridge to the park boundary. Therefore, the most intensive stocking occurs there, and fishing is always excellent. Incredibly fantastic fishing for smallmouth bass is found in this and the Tuckasegee rivers, especially in the lower reaches of the 'Luftee.

Angling pressure downstream from the US 19W bridge to the river's confluence with the Tuckasegee is scant, according to Adam Thompson, a long-time veteran with the tribe's fishery program and a member of the Eastern Band of Cherokee. "Not many people fish down there because they don't think that area holds trout, and access is a little more difficult. There, the river is slower and looks deeper. This stops some from going downstream," he says.

"This area isn't stocked as heavily as other easy-to-get-to places, but it does hold a lot of big trout, especially brown trout. Were I looking for a big trout, I'd try there, and I'd probably use a 5- to

7-inch creek chub for bait, long-line fishing it into a deep, dark pool very early in the morning or in very late evening," notes Thompson. He has probably seen more fishermen catch the biggest trout of their careers than any other man alive.

Access: US 441 traces alongside the river's eastern bank from the Park boundary downstream to the river's confluence with Soco Creek. Big Cove Road lends access to the river's eastern bank downstream to where this road has a junction with US 19W, which lends additional access to the Oconaluftee River down-stream from the town of Cherokee to the reservation's boundary at Birdstown. Access to the river's other side is provided by a road-way known as Old #4.

Soco Creek

SIZE: Small to medium
FISHING PRESSURE: Heavy
FISHING QUALITY: Excellent
ACCESS: US 19W
USGS QUADS: Sylva North, NC; Whittier, NC

Soco Creek is the only significant streamshed beginning within the confines of the Cherokee Indian Reservation. Its origins are between mile-high Soco Bald (5,440 feet in elevation) and Waterrock Knob Mountain (6,292 feet in elevation), which form a steep-walled series of ridges that divide Oconaluftee and Maggie valleys. Unlike its sister peak to the west, Soco Mountain is home to many people, despite its rugged character and steep terrain.

Compared to other Qualla Reservation streams like the Oconaluftee River or Raven Fork, Soco Creek is quite small. Its headwater reaches are pleasant and tree-lined; however, its final three miles, though adequate and providing good fishing, lag behind other Cherokee streams in aesthetics. Soco Creek's head-water reaches are small, but a generous helping of cascades and pools amidst the shade of towering streamside hemlocks and dense-growing laurel make it appealing.

Soco Creek is large enough to permit fly-fishing, but more than 90 percent of all angling occurring here involves the use of natural baits. Top spots include those deep pools (particularly those near the road or along a well-beaten path) and stretches of stream near access road crossings. This is not meant to discredit other areas, because they certainly hold large numbers of fish, especially "smart" holdover trout.

Upstream from Soco Creek's junction with Hornbuckle Creek, approximately 10 miles upstream from its mouth at the Oconaluftee River just downstream from the town of Cherokee, this stream is restricted to tribal members. Although Soco Creek is fed by two impressive feeder streams, Wright and Jenkins creeks, these flows are not open to public fishing under the Enterprise Waters program. It is also worth noting that a very small section of Soco Creek downstream from the US 441 bridge, to that point where the creek again flows adjacent to the reservation, in places is partially under tribal control, while one section of approximately 50 feet is under the control of the state of North Carolina. This area is well-marked, but pay attention to which section of the stream you are in when choosing to fish there.

Access: Access to Soco Creek is excellent, with US 19W providing the bulk of this access. This federal asphalt way closely follows the stream's course for approximately 8 miles to the second bridge just upstream from the town of Cherokee. There, the creek makes a 1.4-mile loop around a sloping ridge, skirting under US 441 before merging with the Oconaluftee River. No roads provide access to this loop area, but enough anglers explore it to keep a footpath open along this reach.

US 19W follows Soco Creek very closely in most sections, although it does lose sight of the creek in places. Numerous side roads lend additional access to those areas away from this highway, and because Soco Creek, like all Enterprise Waters, is heavily fished, well-worn footpaths trace the creek's course.

Stream Index